Only Women Understand

Other books by Lorraine Bodger

2,001 Ways to Pamper Yourself

For You, My Friend, I Wish . . .

For Your Birthday, I Wish . . .

511 Things Only Women Understand

Lorraine Bodger

Andrews McMeel Publishing

Kansas City

 For information, write Andrews McMeel Publishing, an Andrews McMeel Universal company, 4520 Main Street, Kansas City, Missouri 64111.

ISBN: 0-7407-1406-6

Library of Congress Catalog Card Number: 00-108471

Book design by Lisa Martin
Illustrations by Lorraine Bodger

Introduction

You know it, he knows it, your best friend knows it: There are some things that only women understand. We can't help it—we were raised that way. It just goes with the territory. If you're a woman, you know exactly what I mean. If you're not . . . well, only women understand these things.

The way women think is different from the way men think, even now as we head into the twenty-first century. We're observant, intuitive, empathetic, and devastatingly smart. We try to explain why and how we know what we know, and guys stare at us blankly, scratching their heads: Where did that idea come from? What does she mean by that? How did she come to that conclusion?

But women know precisely what other women mean. We hear the loud ring of the familiar and a thousand-watt bulb pops on: Yes, yes, yes, I know *just* what she's talking about. Men, much as we love them, simply don't get it—and that's one reason we're so attached to our female friends: They do.

Therefore, ladies, prepare for the pleasure of instant recognition. Curl up with 511 I-didn't-really-have-to-tell-you-this-because-you-already-knew-it items of not-so-secret information. Everybody's welcome to read them. Just don't ask us to explain.

Only women understand . . .

• 1 •

The alarming difference between 120 pounds and 121 pounds.

• 2 •

Why you're allowed to have guy friends, but he's not allowed to have women friends.

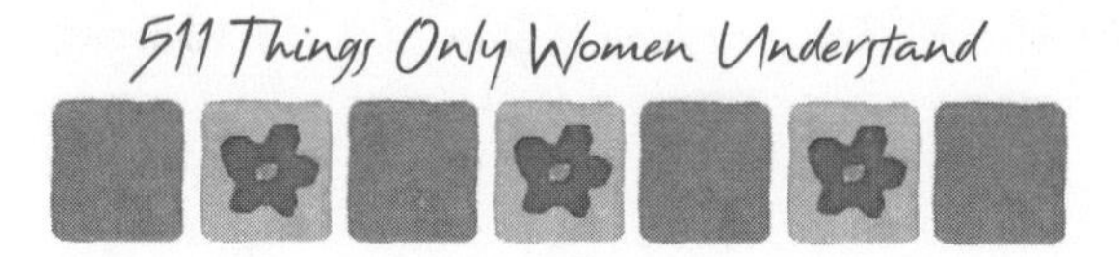

• 3 •

That friendships can be as
comfy as old sweatshirts,
but love affairs shouldn't be.

• 4 •

Why you need your own
a) bank account
b) credit card
c) bathroom
d) closet
e) all of the above

·5·

Why sex is better if
you're awake, too.

·6·

How to fold laundry correctly.

·7·

How to pack the trunk
of the car correctly.

How to set the table correctly.

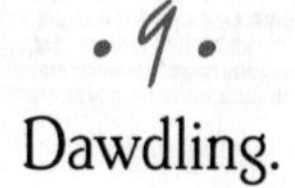

Dawdling.

•10•

The tone of your girlfriend's telephone voice when she means: He's in the room, so I can't talk about *that* right now.

• 11 •

The difference between pants, regular pants, nice pants, good pants, and dressy pants.

· 12 ·

Why it makes perfect sense to wear toe-crushing, arch-defying, exquisitely beautiful pumps.

· 13 ·

The Great Divide: women with kids and women without.

· 14 ·

What it is exactly about mice . . .

• 15 •

That the noise in the cellar in the middle of the night is not the house settling. It is an ax murderer or, at the very least, a large, scary robber.

• 16 •

How to make cookies come off the cookie sheet.

• 17 •

Being addicted to women's magazines.

• 18 •

That it's all very well to have a good husband, but if you don't have a good

a) hair colorist

b) aerobics instructor

c) car mechanic

d) baby-sitter

e) all of the above

you might as well be dead.

• 19 •

Why you need a new
winter coat even though
last year's isn't worn out.

That you're allowed to read in
bed with a light on when he's
trying to go to sleep,
but he isn't because
the light keeps
you awake.

• 21 •

That you're allowed to leave hair in the sink and on the soap, but he isn't because it makes you sick.

• 22 •

That he's not allowed to leave underwear all over the bedroom, but you are because your underwear is prettier.

·23·

A filing system based on intuitive logic: Old letters from your mother are filed under CATASTROPHES, and old love letters are filed (naturally) under IMPORTANT DOCUMENTS.

·24·

How maddening it is to
hear only the sound of babies
and children all day long.
So maddening that you find
yourself calling a radio talk
show just to exchange a few
words with a human being
over the age of four.

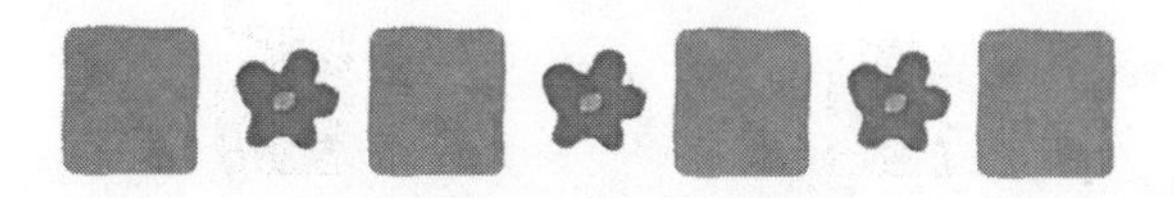

• 25 •

That the photograph you have taken for your passport, driver's license, or ID will be the worst one you've ever seen.

Why you want him to hold the door for you.

• 27 •

Why you don't want him to hold the door for you.

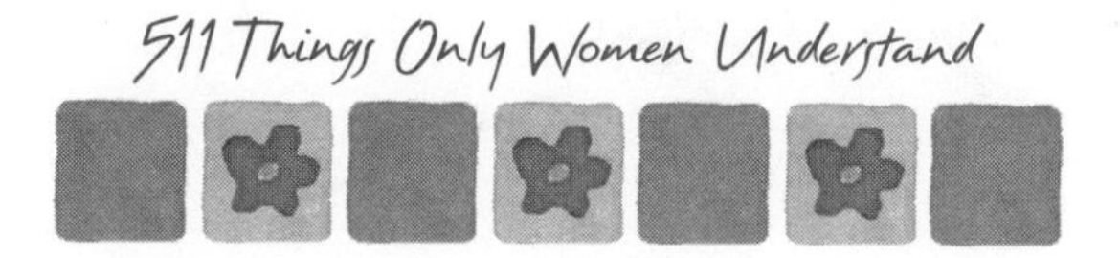

·28·

The subtle gradations of friendship:
You'd tell that story to *her* but not to *her*.

That the cat is yours
and the dog is his.

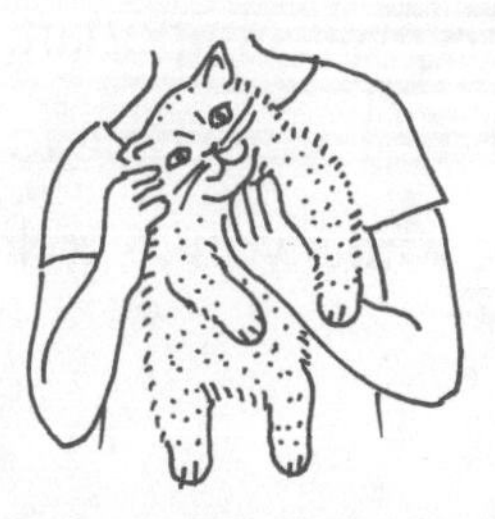

• 30 •

The heart-stopping
thrill of a sale on
cashmere sweaters.

• 31 •

That your office Christmas
party is just as important as his,
and he'd better come to yours
if he wants you to go to his.

• 32 •

The ability to ignore
that great big groan or
squeak from your car.

The inability to ignore
even that teeny-tiny groan or
squeak from your baby.

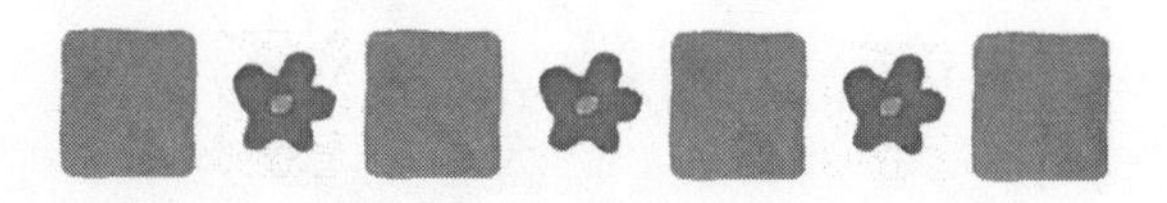

·34·

Why a woman cannot have too many pairs of black slacks.

Why it is not flattering to be called

a) chubbykins
b) my little plumpkin
c) a nice handful
d) Big Mama
e) any of the above

•36•

The difference between
dry housework
(changing a lightbulb)
and wet housework
(cleaning the bathroom),
and why women usually
get stuck with the wet kind.

•37•

Lip bleach. Hot wax. Tweezing.

• 38 •

Why food tastes better
when eaten with an actual fork,
from a plate, on a table,
with a place mat and napkin.

• 39 •

Why it would be fun to go
to Europe this year for your
vacation instead of going back to
the rustic cabin (the one with the
outhouse) by the trout stream.

• 40 •

How to look as if you're listening attentively while you're actually planning your grocery list in your head.

• 41 •

The difference between taupe, toast, mocha, café au lait, bark, cinnamon, auburn, chestnut, walnut, sepia, and umber.

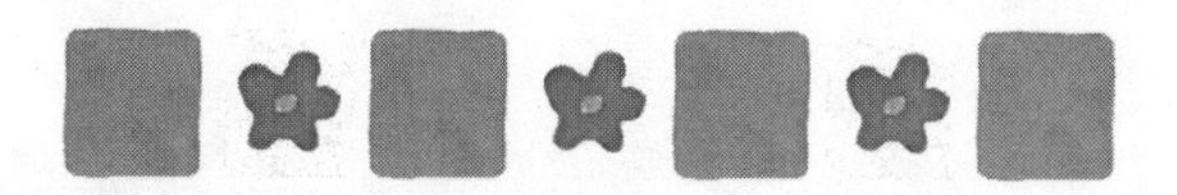

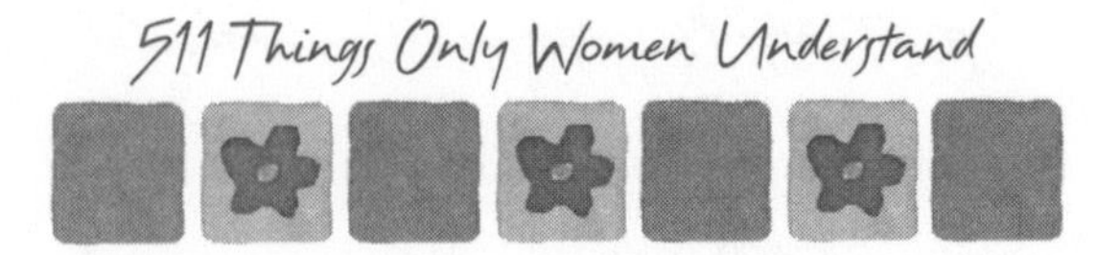

• 42 •

Why a week's worth of panty hose dries better when allowed to hang from the shower curtain rod.

• 43 •

That a bouquet of roses, though delightful, is not a substitute for doing the chores he was supposed to do.

• 44 •

That calling fifteen minutes before the two of you are supposed to leave for a dinner party, in order to tell you he'll be an hour late, is not amusing.

• 45 •

That listening—really listening—to a woman is the sexiest thing a man can do.

•46•

Why it's essential
to pack your makeup case
in your carry-on bag,
not in your luggage.

•47•

When to be honest
and when to lie.

·48·

The Internet: Networking and multitasking are exactly the same things you've always done, but you used to call them keeping in touch and doing ten things at the same time.

• 49 •

That there is a glass ceiling.

• 50 •

Why you can't tolerate his

a) mother

b) sister

c) best guy friend

d) old girlfriend

e) all of the above

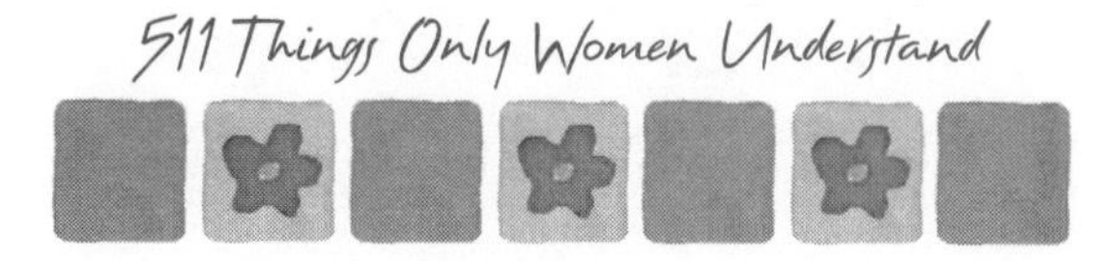

•51•

That the way to make
the phone ring is to go
to the bathroom.

•52•

The importance of
excellent diplomatic relations—
with the plumber, the dry cleaner,
the vet, the mail carrier,
the UPS driver, and every
other life-support system.

• 53 •

Silver nail polish.

• 54 •

That the answer to the question *Who stays home when the kids are sick?* should not be an automatic *She does.*

How to put on lipstick with a mouth full of Novocain.

·56·

The subtle gradations of flirting: A friendly smile across the table at lunch means one thing, but if you lean *toward* him when you smile at him, that's something else entirely.

·57·

The correct way to minister to someone with an extremely bad case of flu.

• 58 •

That life is not a soap opera.
Most of the time.

• 59 •

The crucial difference
between a good haircut
and a great one.

• 60 •

Why it is uncompromisingly necessary for you to put on your makeup before setting foot outside the house: If you go out with a bare face, you will absolutely bump into your old college sweetheart.

• 61 •

That the opportunity to wear your new outfit is a reason to go on living.

·62·

Cinderella. Snow White.
The Ugly Duckling.

·63·

The overwhelming urge to try to please *everyone*—and the impossibility of doing so.

The telltale signs of cheapness in a man:

• saving rubber bands

• giving you a gift without gift wrap

• bringing bad wine to a dinner party

• insisting that the generic brand of everything is just as good

• a subtle hesitation when the waiter brings the check

• arriving so late at the movies that you've already bought the tickets

• 65 •

That finding a pair of perfectly fitting jeans approaches having a religious experience.

That personality is revealed by one's choice of underwear.

• 67 •

The difference between
a girl and a woman.

• 68 •

That you become invisible
the day you turn fifty.

• 69 •

The overwhelming urge to
apologize even when you haven't
done anything wrong.

·70·

That a year or two of having to repeat yourself three or four times whenever you say something to your guy just might be a deal breaker.

·71·

The arrangement of food in the pantry, or Why the cat food goes behind the peanut butter, which is next to the tea bags, which are balanced on the jar of salsa.

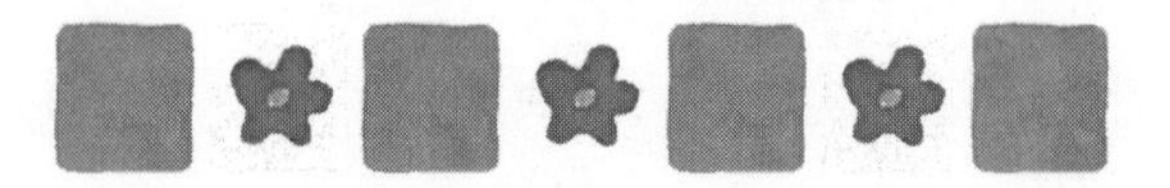

• 72 •

The arrangement of pots and pans in the kitchen, or Why some of the saucepans go under the counter near the stove and others go across the room in a cupboard, and the lids are nowhere near either.

• 73 •

The heartbreak of stretch marks, varicose veins, cottage cheese thighs, and fat knees.

• 74 •

When to press your dearest friend to tell you what's wrong—and when to wait for her to bring it up herself.

• 75 •

That you want him to go to your high school reunion with you.

• 76 •

That you don't want him to go to your high school reunion with you.

• 77 •

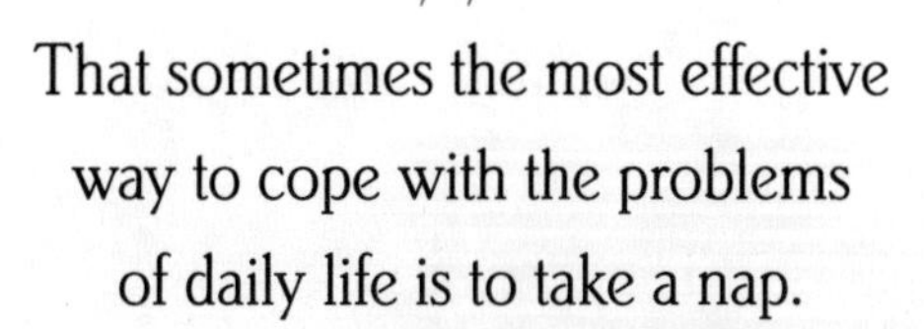

That sometimes the most effective way to cope with the problems of daily life is to take a nap.

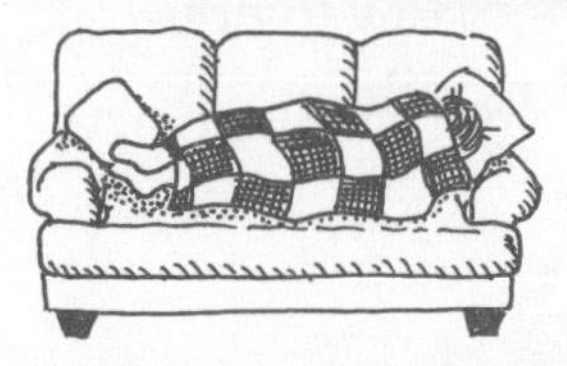

• 78 •

How to drive a man crazy.

• 79 •

How to drive another woman crazy.

• 80 •

How to drive your mother crazy.

How to get your father to
come over and fix the sink.

Why a vacuum cleaner is
not a good birthday present
for a woman. Same goes for
a humidifier, a lawn mower,
or an electric toothbrush.
A power drill, on the other hand,
might be a breakthrough.

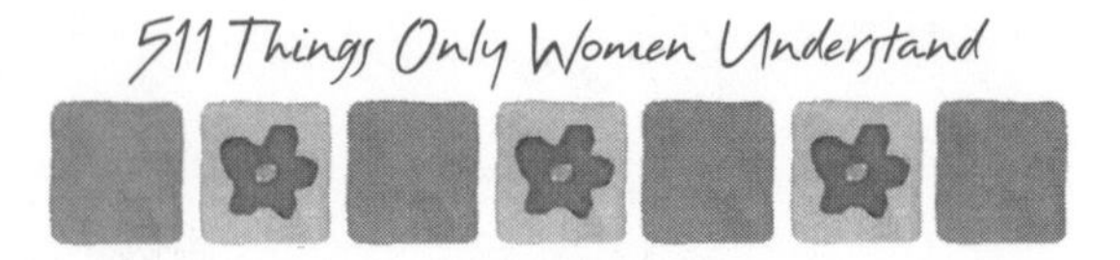

That since you can't do the
bonding thing with your male boss
in the steam room or the locker
room, you'd better find an
alternative venue—fast—
if you want to keep up.

• 84 •

That since you can do
the bonding thing with your
female boss in the gym,
the spa, or the ladies' room,
take advantage of it.

If he says he doesn't deserve you, he probably doesn't. And if he says you're too good for him, you probably are.

• 86 •

Why it's necessary to change the sheets at least once a week.

• 87 •

Ditto the towels.

That getting dressed each day won't be a crisis if you care a *lot* about clothes (in which case you don't mind shopping, coordinating, and all the rest of it) or if you care not at all about clothes (in which case clean underwear, a T-shirt, and a pair of jeans will get you through life).

·89·

That there's something basically wrong when the majority of politicians are male in a country where the majority of people are female.

·90·

Why it's better not to tell a soul when you go on a diet.

• 91 •

That when he says
he'll call you soon, he won't.
But when he says
he'll call you tomorrow
at seven-thirty, he will.

• 92 •

That men use things up and do not replace them. This includes paper towels, dental floss, Pepto-Bismol, shampoo, milk, cookies, laundry detergent, stamps, printer paper, copier paper, and toilet paper.

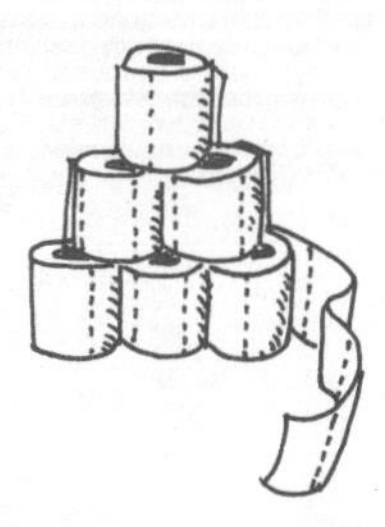

• 93 •

The difference between
a dish towel and a rag:
Do not use the dish towel
to polish the car.
Do not shine shoes with it.
Do not use it to catch paint drips.

• 94 •

That making a list of the things you have to do is almost as good as doing them.

• 95 •

Why erotica for women is different from erotica for men.

• 96 •

That the older you get,
the better your clothes should be.
Leave the cheap flash to the
twenty-somethings.

• 97 •

That regardless of what your
husband chooses to believe, it
wasn't your imagination: His best
friend *did* try to flirt with you.

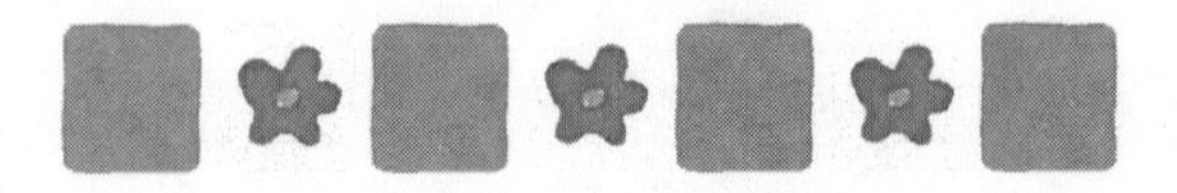

Where the household
budget *really* goes.

That men get too much
credit for being monogamous,
and women get too little.

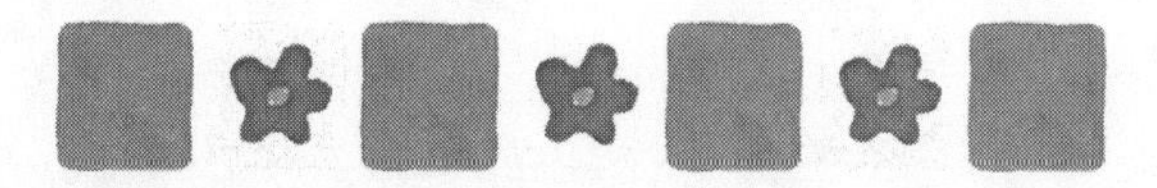

• 100 •

Certain movies:

Thelma & Louise

Hanging Up

Steel Magnolias

9 to 5

Diary of a Mad Housewife

Waiting to Exhale

Moonstruck

• 101 •

Obsessing over your
biological clock.

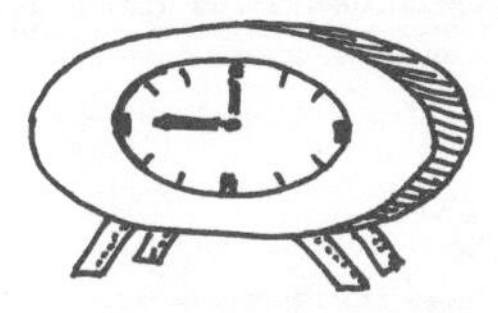

• 102 •

Changing your mind
fifteen times in an hour.

• 103 •

That when you're out of sorts or depressed, the best quick remedy is to call a friend. (Men would sooner call the dentist.)

• 104 •

When you doll yourself up and go to a party, it will drive you nuts if the men huddle together in a corner and ignore you.

• 105 •

That the clothes in the fashion magazines are chosen by delusional editors who have lost touch with reality and no longer know (or care) what normal women can afford or would dream of wearing.

• 106 •

That people who don't ask you any questions about yourself after you've asked ten questions about them aren't good material for dates, friendship, or anything else.

• 107 •

Why it's unhelpful for your boyfriend or husband to point out that you've gone off your diet when you have.

• 108 •

That having many, many, many pairs of shoes does not make you a foot fetishist.

·109·

How to program the VCR so you'll be sure to miss the show you meant to tape.

·110·

How to make a meal out of any three ingredients you find in the refrigerator.

• 111 •

Rubber gloves.

• 112 •

The ecstasy of still fitting into your wedding dress ten years later.

• 113 •

Buying that perfect T-shirt in five different colors.

• 114 •

That no matter how gender-neutral you become, you'll never be able to change a flat tire.

• 115 •

That no matter how gender-neutral you become, you'll never want to spend an entire evening discussing professional hockey.

• 116 •

That no matter how gender-neutral you become, you'll never agree to stop painting your toenails.

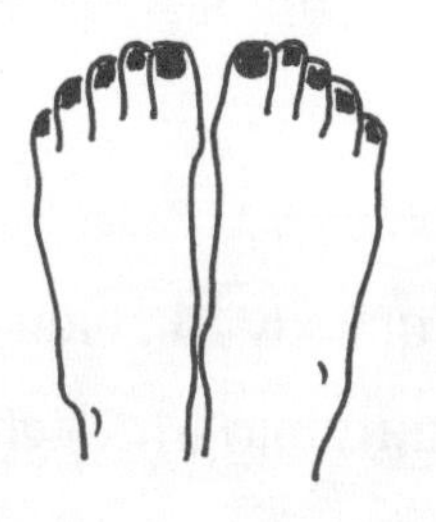

• 117 •

Why you need your own special shampoo even though the hotel provides loads of little bottles of the stuff.

• 118 •

How quickly Mr. Generosity can turn into Mr. Tightwad after the wedding.

· 119 ·

How you can love and loathe your

a) mother

b) father

c) sister

d) brother

e) husband

at the same time.

•120•

The unbeatable combination of girlfriends and a kitchen table.

•121•

Jacks. Double Dutch. Cat's cradle.

•122•

That men don't know how to talk about problems until we teach them.

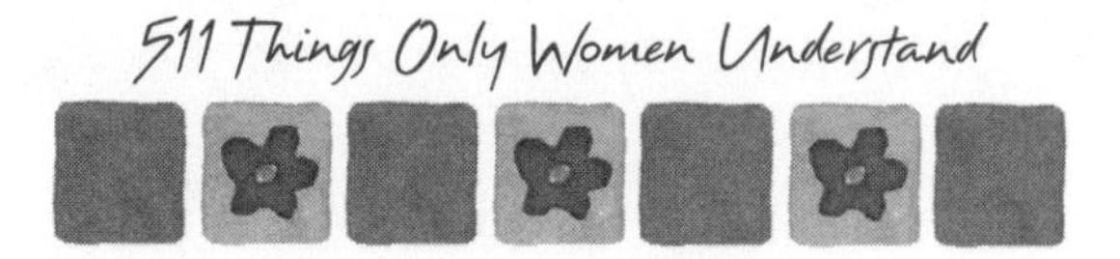

• 123 •

How endearing it is when a man remembers your favorite color, flower, author, rock band, sandwich, and flavor of ice cream.

• 124 •

That when you're out on a date it's a turn-on to pick up the check. (Hey, sport, that's one reason men like to do it.)

·125·

Why you're allowed to keep all those funky old outfits you'll never wear again, but he has to throw out the checked suits with the wide lapels, the Nehru jackets, the nylon shirts with the jungle prints, and anything that even vaguely resembles what his father wears.

· 126 ·

That spending $50 on a sweater marked down from $150 means you have an extra $100 in your checking account.

· 127 ·

It's easier to split the bill than do the math, and it all comes out right in the end anyway.

•128•

Why it's tempting to defer your own needs when there are eight million demands on your time. And why it's essential not to.

•129•

That men do not speak the same language women speak, even when it sounds like standard English.

• 130 •

How alarming it can feel
to fly into a rage—
and then how great it can
feel to yell and act out.

• 131 •

How to handle rejection.
Right.

• 132 •

That fathers have some input in the baby-making process, but mothers do most of the real work.

· 133 ·

Why Girls' Night Out
is not on the list of optionals.

That older men going out
with younger women are
searching desperately for youth,
but older women going out with
younger men are searching
desperately for equals.

• 135 •

His parents would like some private time *with* him, *without* you. And that's why you're not visiting the in-laws today.

• 136 •

That contrary to what your married-with-kids offspring think, being a grandmother (and baby-sitting) is not the only way you wish to spend your golden years.

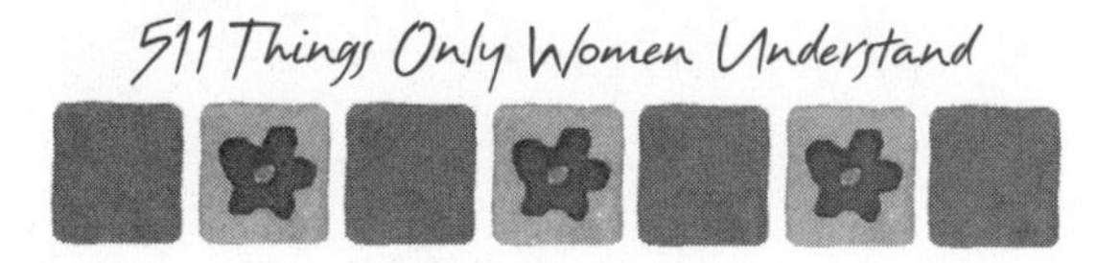

• 137 •

You may have decided to give it up, but you did not *lose* your sexuality when you entered middle age.

If you didn't give it up and haven't lost it, you would like to have your sexuality appreciated *even more* when you enter middle age.

• 139 •

How contact lenses
can change your life—
and not just because
you can see better.

• 140 •

That the safest color
to pick for someone else is,
of course, blue.

• 141 •

That receiving a bouquet of carnations is worse than receiving no bouquet at all.

• 142 •

How to apply makeup in the rearview mirror.

• 143 •

How to function brilliantly
in an emergency.

• 144 •

How to tell a story correctly, with
plenty of interesting digressions.

• 145 •

That we're not making it up:
Bloating is real.

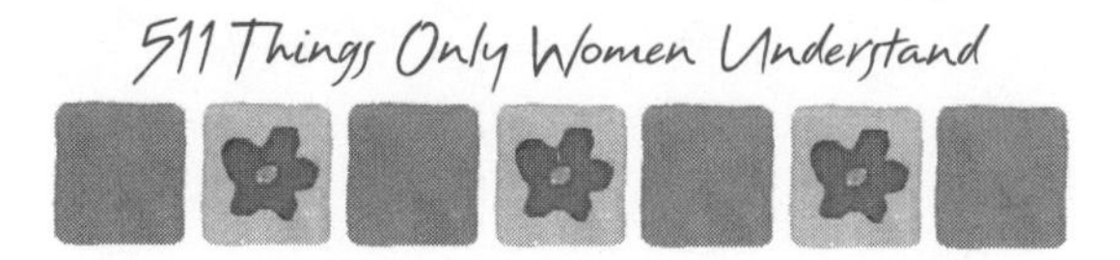

·146·

That if you have to produce one more little kid's birthday party, you're going to put your fist through the piñata.

• 147 •

That the trick for getting things done is *starting* them. Though finishing them is nice, too.

You need hugs and kisses every day. You may not get them, but you need them.

• 149 •

The rules of recycling: You must make a note of who sent you that bilious green tablecloth so you don't inadvertently send it back to her on her next birthday.

• 150 •

Men's haircuts: There's a world of difference between a good one and the one he gets at the corner barbershop.

• 151 •

Amortization: If you wear that three-hundred-dollar suede jacket thirty times, it costs only ten dollars per wearing.

• 152 •

Why it's probably better to date before you go to bed with someone.

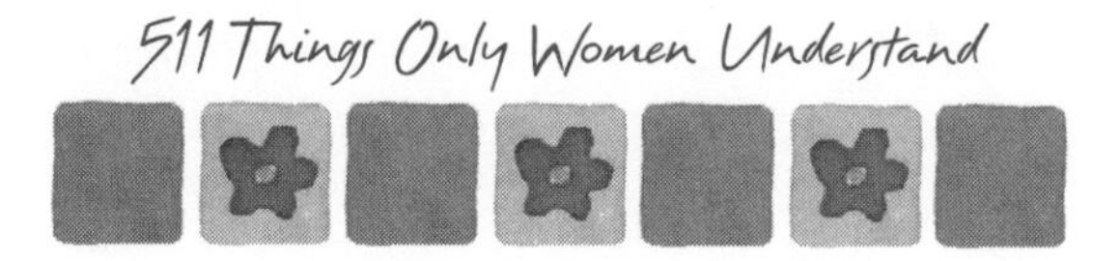

• 153 •

That using the last yard
of toilet paper without replacing
the roll is barbaric.

• 154 •

It's far, far better to be called
vain than to be called selfish,
boring, or stupid. Or is it the
other way around?

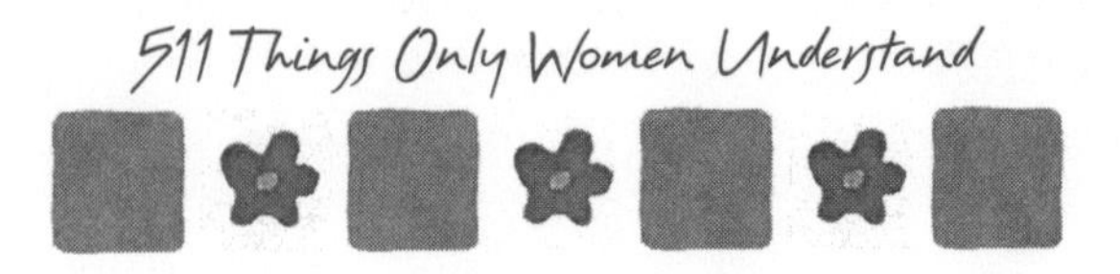

• 155 •

That it's just about the
most annoying thing in the
world when a man you meet
at a party asks, right off the bat,
what your husband does—
instead of asking what *you* do.

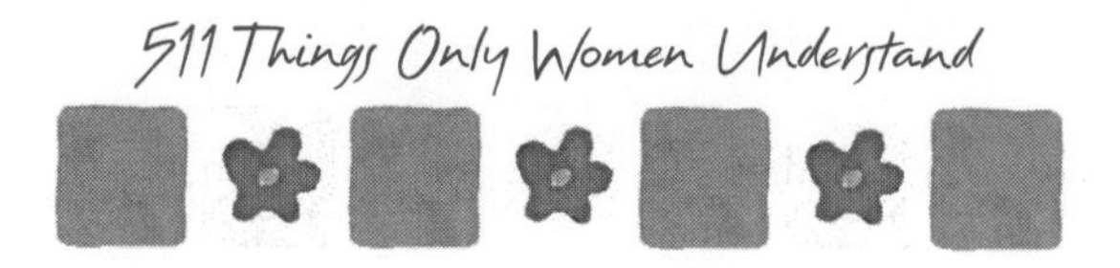

•156•

The importance of
slowing down. Even if you
can't manage to do it.

•157•

That there are some men who
will never see you as anything
but a pretty face, and they're
the ones you shouldn't be
married to or working for.

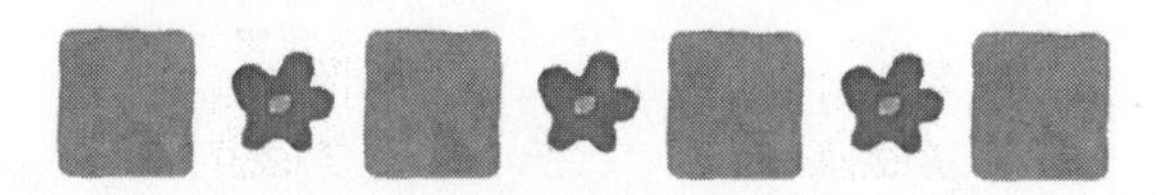

• 158 •

That the professional organizers and planners are actually in a conspiracy to *waste* your time, not save it. Does any family truly need color-coded socks? Or alphabetized canned goods?

• 159 •

How to wrap a present so it doesn't look as if a two-year-old did it.

• 160 •

That it takes you about one millisecond to detect a woman who doesn't like other women.

• 161 •

How to end the shouting
and start the talking.

That all the smart-money tricks
in the world will not, in the end,
prevent you from putting that
pair of sexy, strappy, faux-alligator
high-heeled sandals on your
overworked credit card.

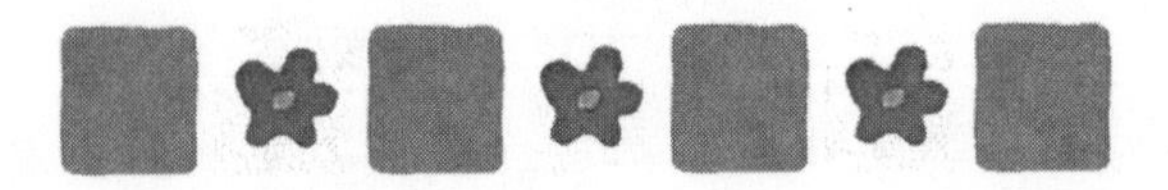

• 163 •

That you may have honorably earned every fine line and crease you have on your face, but who wants to be paid in wrinkles?

• 164 •

Why your husband should reward you with an eighteen-inch diamond necklace after you have a baby. But you'll settle for diamond studs.

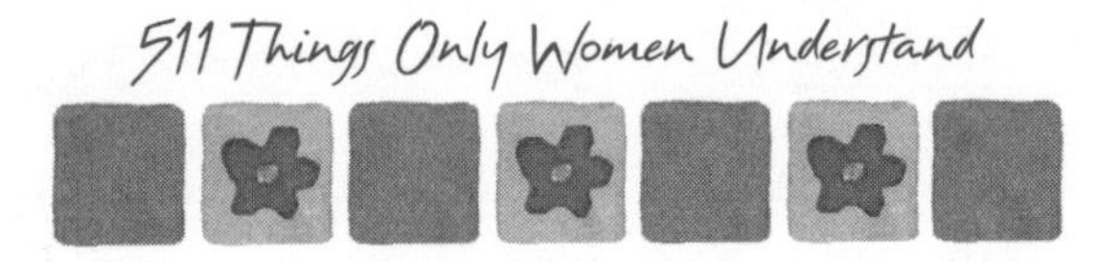

•165•

That the efficient way to avoid unpleasant domestic chores is to sit right down and give yourself a beautiful new manicure. Then it will be out of the question to ruin those gorgeous nails by mucking out the garage, won't it?

• 166 •

Why you would prefer
to leave the house during

a) football games
b) wall demolition
c) karaoke practice
d) software installation
e) tax preparation (unless *you're* doing it, in which case you'd prefer him to leave) and come back when things have returned to normal.

• 167 •

That running out of coffee, panty hose, mascara, and gas on the same morning is enough to send you back to bed for the rest of the day.

• 168 •

That the mirrors in the clothing store changing rooms are specially designed and manufactured to make you look the worst you possibly can.

• 169 •

Why women do not like
to be teased about their bodies,
particularly in bed.

• 170 •

Why pockets will never
replace handbags. (Try carrying
Tampax in your pocket.)

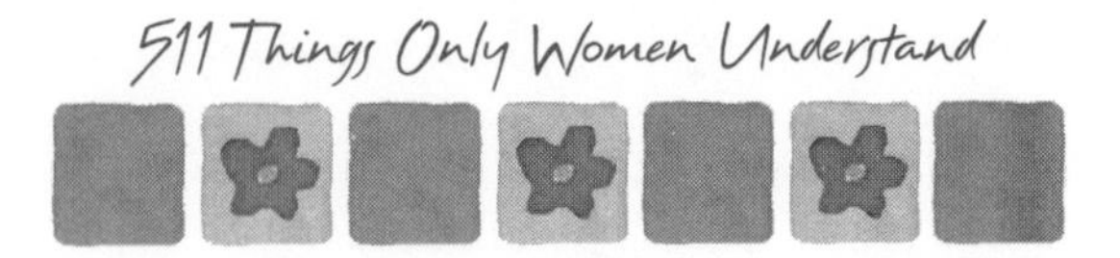

• 171 •

How irritating it is when total strangers pat your pregnant belly and ask when the baby's due.

How infuriating it is when total strangers give you child-rearing advice when you're minding your own business at the playground.

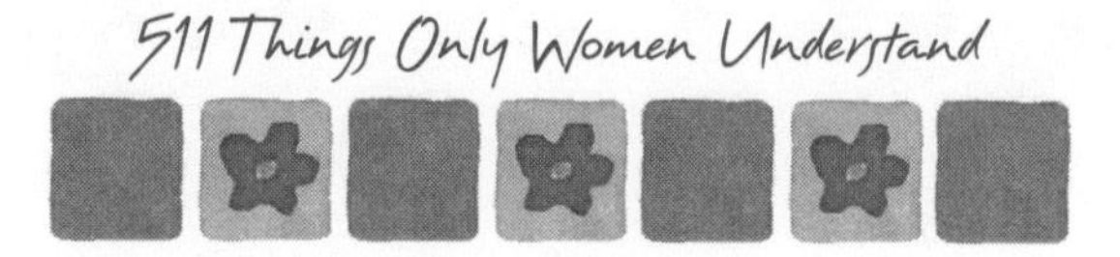

• 173 •

How enraging it is when the blue-haired dowagers frown and tsk-tsk as your child is having a tantrum in the supermarket. (Do they think you're enjoying those bloodcurdling screams?)

·174·

That discussing your nervous breakdown, your hunky personal trainer, or the financial settlement in your divorce is not good first-date strategy.

·175·

That girls can enjoy baseball and boys can enjoy dolls. No big deal.

• 176 •

It's possible to have it all,
but not all at once.

The luxury of letting someone
else take a turn at calling the
electrician, accountant,
exterminator, insurance company,
or telephone repair service.

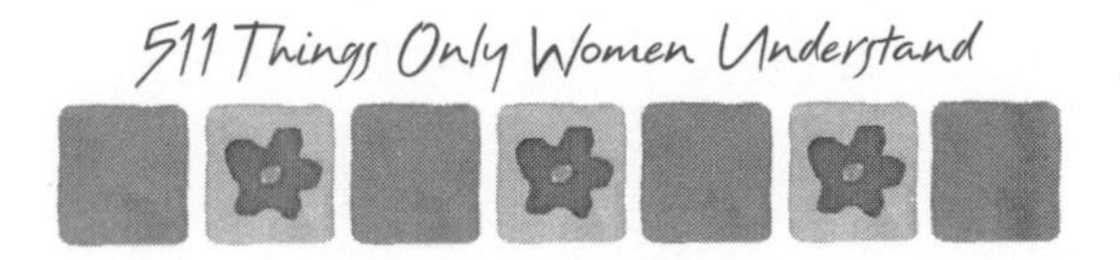

• 178 •

How to spend
a day relaxing in bed
without having sex.

Why it's so satisfying
to go on an occasional
crying jag.

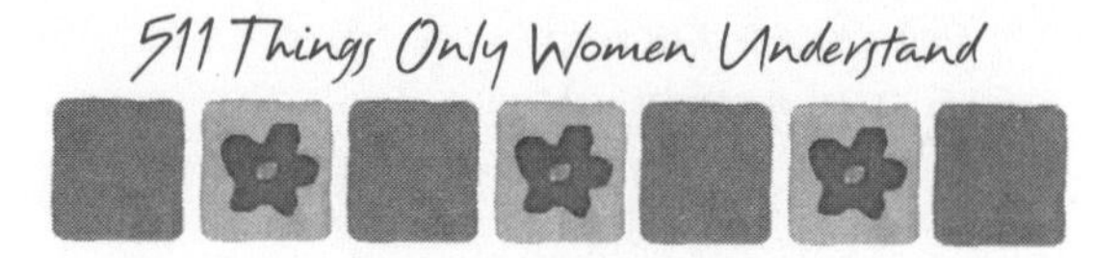

• 180 •

That it does not bode well if the man you're going out with eats exactly the same breakfast, lunch, and dinner every single day of the week.

• 181 •

That stopping along the way at little shops, tag sales, and roadside stands is half the point of taking the journey. (Why do men think that getting there is the whole point?)

·182·

That when you want some escape time, you'd rather go to a romantic comedy than an action, disaster, martial arts, or horror movie.

·183·

Why hanging a dirty shirt in the closet for a week will not make it wearable again.

• 184 •

That iced latte with sugar
and a sprinkling of cocoa
powder is a diet drink.
Par excellence.

•185•

Why self-service gas stations are not an improvement on full-service ones.

How much you hate hearing about all the attractive women he admires on the street when you're out together.

• 187 •

The sexiness of older men:

Gene Hackman

Nelson Mandela

Tony Bennett

the Buena Vista Social Club

• 188 •

The thrill of a bra

that fits perfectly.

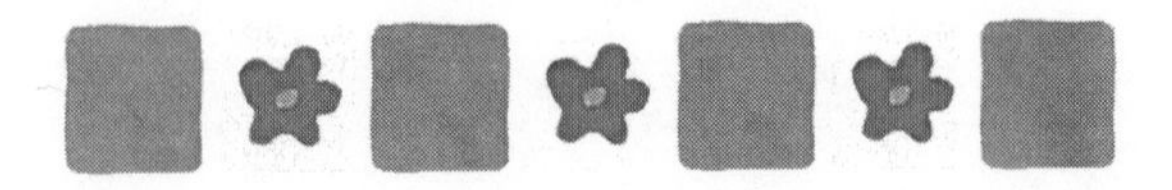

•189•

The thrill of a really great nightgown.

•190•

Exfoliation.

• 191 •

The tyranny of the to-do list.

• 192 •

If you expended as much effort planning and carrying out all the great activities that the books and magazines recommend for your children, you'd have to hire someone else to be their mother.

· 193 ·

That fancy new kitchen appliances do not save time and work. They only *take* time and *make* work. There's a good reason why that pasta maker, waffle iron, ice shaver, juice extractor, and bread machine end up gathering dust in the pantry.

• 194 •

That historically women have often had to work twice as hard in the office to get the same amount of attention, kudos, respect, and money as the guy at the next desk. It's past time to change history.

• 195 •

Seesawing between wanting to smooth the path for your grown-up kids and wanting to let them make their own way, for their own good.

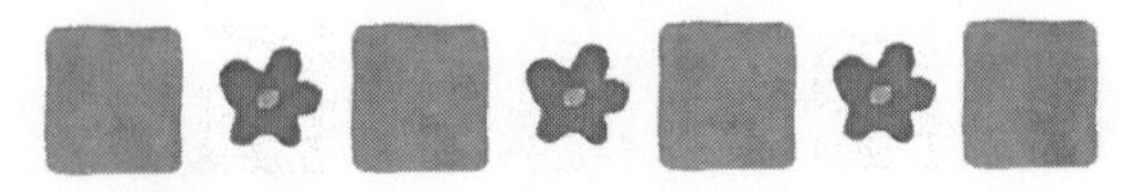

• 196 •

The critical importance
of telling a girlfriend if

• her fly is unzipped
• her mascara is running
• there's a smudge on her nose
• she has lipstick on her front tooth

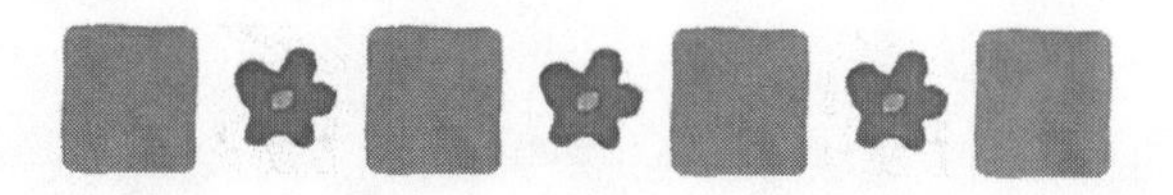

• 197 •

That high-gloss black tiles and black fixtures are absolutely out of the question in the master bathroom, no matter how cool he thinks they are.

• 198 •

The value of thinking before responding.

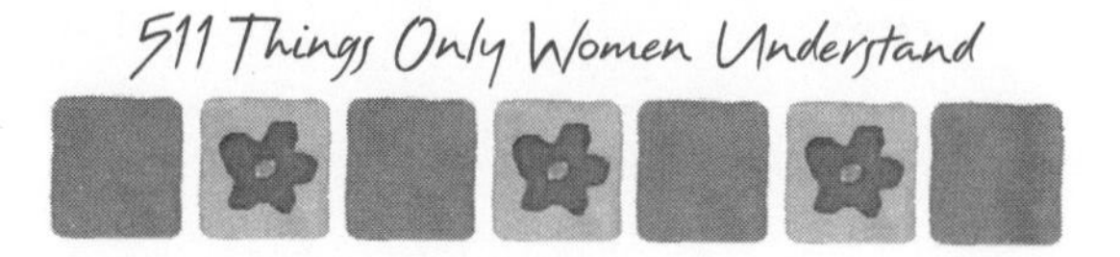

• 199 •

Charm bracelets. Tote bags.
High-heeled boots.

• 200 •

The impossibility of getting in and out of the backseat of a two-door car gracefully.

• 201 •

That it's fun to be spontaneous about things other than sex.

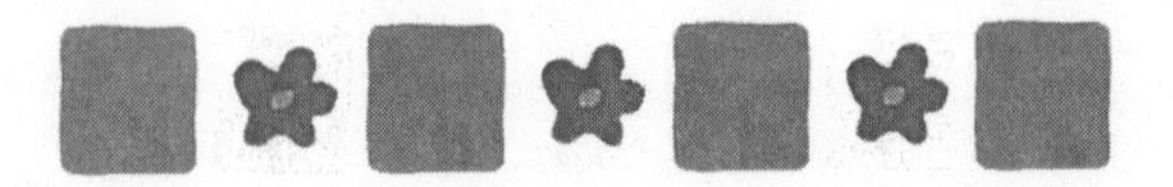

• 202 •

That the milk crate planter and the recycled tablecloth curtains that were so adorable in the women's magazine will look like an old box and a pair of rags when you put them in your own home.

• 203 •

That even if your guy never lies about anything, he couldn't possibly mean it when he says you look just as good without makeup as with it.

• 204 •

Why we can be good to everyone but ourselves.

· 205 ·

Why we can stand up for
our best friends and co-workers
but not for ourselves.

· 206 ·

That when a man wants to go
to a topless beach, it's probably
not for the sun and surf.

• 207 •

That a Mother's Day gift,
though nice, is only a small drop
in a very large bucket.

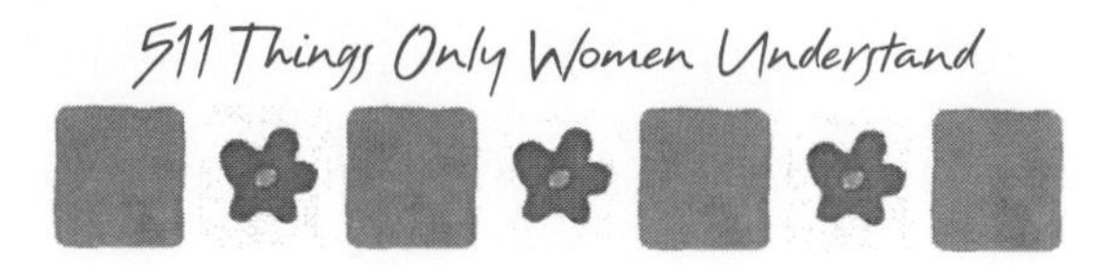

·208·

How to find an ATM at any hour of the day or night.

·209·

Taking a month to find the right shoes and handbag.

·210·

The girlfriend phone network.

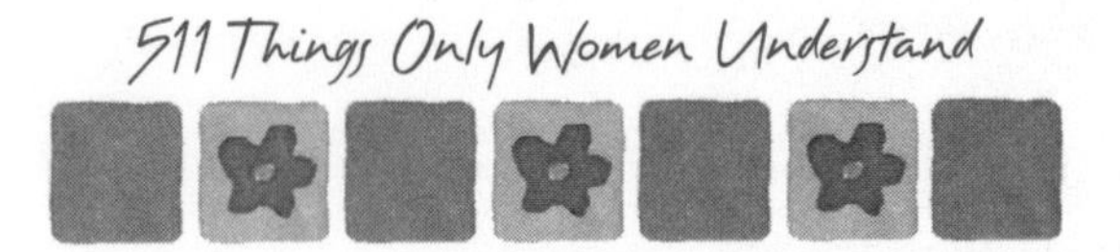

• 211 •

That short of sperm donation, there's almost no such thing as men's work or women's work anymore.

• 212 •

Playing dress-up. Even when you're a full-grown adult.

• 213 •

That the efficiency experts are always doling out advice that every sane woman has known forever. Do they really think you need to be told to buy in bulk? Or to throw out the clothes you don't wear?

• 214 •

That when you need to keep a meeting or a visit brief, *you* must go to *her* office or home so you can leave whenever you want.

• 215 •

The difference between short shorts and hot pants.

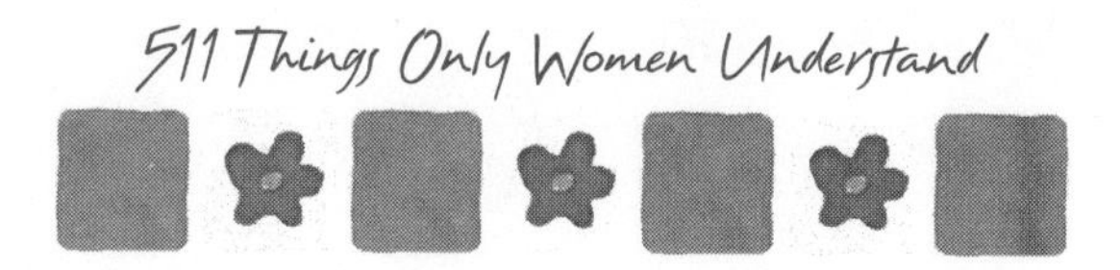

• 216 •

What the most important appliance in the house is: the bathroom scale.

• 217 •

What the second most important appliance in the house is: the bathroom scale.

• 218 •

Having a temper tantrum over a nail that breaks ten minutes after a manicure.

• 219 •

That boys and men get away with murder when it comes to using foul language *to* and *about* girls and women. Sorry, but it's true.

•220•

That a mother's life may soon have to be lived (if it isn't already) with one hand clutching a child and the other clutching a Palm Pilot.

•221•

Baby shower etiquette.

• 222 •

How hard it is to say no to

- the PTA Bake Sale committee
- the block association
- someone who insists on helping you when you don't want help
- a friend who's too clingy
- the telephone pollster
- your mother
- your boss

• 223 •

The total fun of trying
on clothes, shoes, and jewelry
with your best girlfriend.

• 224 •

How you can have a closet
stuffed to the walls and still not
have anything to wear.

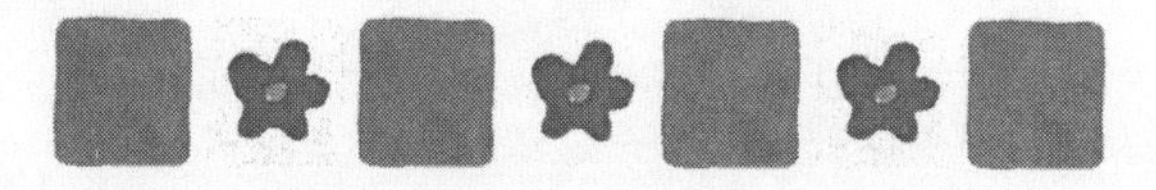

•225•

That where love and sex are concerned, you often have to ask for what you want in order to get it. And sometimes you have to ask more than once.

•226•

The difference between being nice to the man you're dating and being too nice: Kind and considerate is nice. Doing his laundry is too nice.

•227•

How to keep a conversation going.
And going. And going.

Silk. Satin. Velvet. Chiffon.

•229•

Why it might be a good idea
not to learn how to type.

That the following activities are *not* acceptable male excuses for not taking out the garbage:

a) watching the game
b) surfing the Web
c) reading the paper
d) sleeping
e) riding the stationary bicycle

• 231 •

That the following activities are acceptable female excuses for not taking out the garbage:

a) putting on makeup
b) talking on the phone
c) rearranging your shoes
d) reading your e-mail
e) riding the stationary bicycle

•232•

How demoralizing it is the first time someone calls you "ma'am."

The unequivocal disgustingness of worms, slugs, bats, snakes, and jellyfish.

• 234 •

That charm is gender-neutral.

• 235 •

Soccer moms.

• 236 •

Sisters.

• 237 •

The five-day emergency diet. Unfortunately.

·238·

That the people who make the most difference when it comes to women's issues are women.

·239·

That you may be his only best friend, but it's highly unlikely that he's yours.

• 240 •

The shock of discovering that you've aged out of certain clothing stores and departments that you used to shop in all the time.

• 241 •

That women are—
not to put too fine a point upon it—ten thousand times smarter than men.

•242•

Beauty advice: When it says *fast fix*, it means *takes hours.* When it says *simplified*, it means *complicated*. When it says *glow*, it means *shine like an oil slick*. When it says *light scent*, it means *reeking*. When it says *two easy steps*, it means *five hard steps*.

·243·

That there are days when you'd rather be sporting a black leather miniskirt than a black leather briefcase. And vice versa.

·244·

That if every company provided child care on site, off site, or in the form of subsidies, working parents would be a lot happier.

• 245 •

It's only men—not women—
who look back with nostalgia at the
1950s and 1960s, and pine for the
day when husbands ruled the roost.
Or thought they did.

•246•

That *flattering* is not the right word to describe being stalked.

•247•

Why you must meet a blind date in a nice, safe public place.

• 248 •

That there are some
situations in which being
obnoxious is the only appropriate
response—like when
some obnoxious creep
is harassing you.

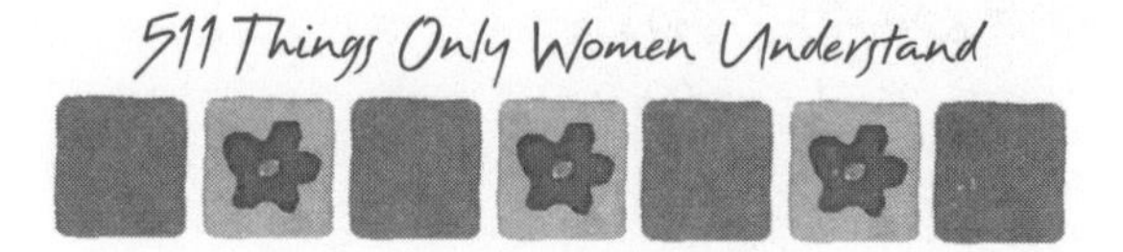

•249•

That juggling a job, home, children, family finances, and social life does not make you Wonder Woman. It makes you Average Woman.

• 250 •

When it's time for you
to stop wearing

a) sleeveless tops
b) stretch pants
c) four-inch heels
d) glitter eye shadow
e) all of the above at the same time

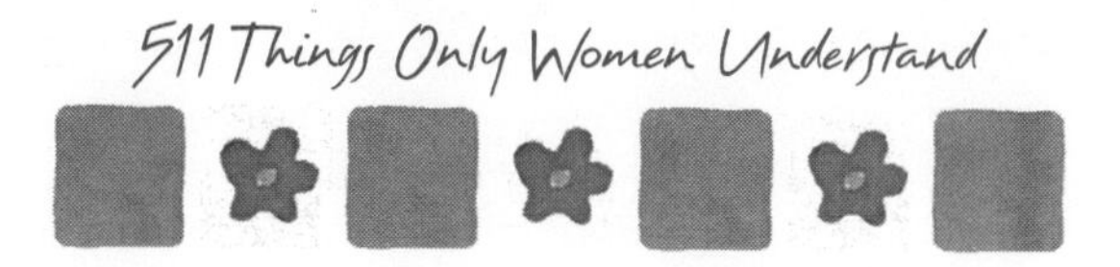

· 251 ·

When it's time for him
to stop wearing

a) muscle T-shirts
b) short shorts
c) kneesocks
d) muttonchop sideburns
e) all of the above at the same time

• 252 •

That many household chores
(ditto papers on your desk)
will go away, become obsolete,
or work themselves out if you
do absolutely nothing at all.

• 253 •

The sexiness of male dancers:
Gregory Hines, Savion Glover,
Mikhail Baryshnikov, Gene Kelly,
Patrick Swayze, Fred Astaire.

• 254 •

Who's having an affair
and who isn't.

•255•

That boyfriends may come and go, but girlfriends are forever.

•256•

Cramps. PMS. Hot flashes.

•257•

What it really means when you're a mature adult and the personnel manager tells you, "Stick to freelancing. Staff jobs are for kids."

·258·

That the stuff they tell you to do to get a man interested in you (like making him feel special and laughing at his jokes) is exactly the same stuff you expect him to do if he wants you to be interested in him. Big surprise.

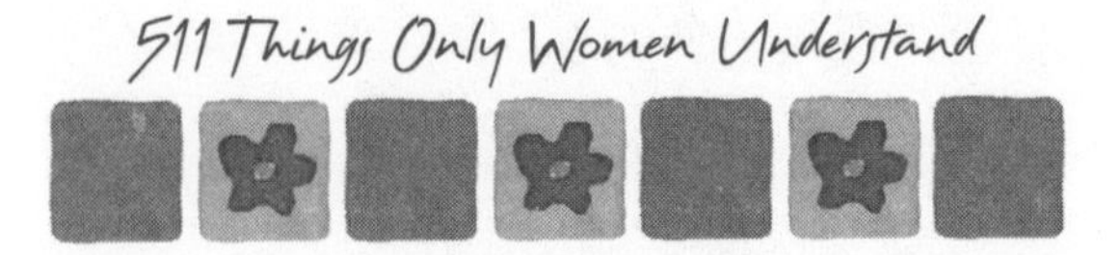

•259•

How a person can live
on yogurt, lettuce, and olives
and still gain weight.

·260·

How to do six things
at once—and do them well.

That being comfortable in your
clothes is not the goal. Looking
good is the goal . . . isn't it?

•262•

The utter delight of having
a fit of the giggles.

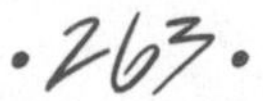

The importance of inventing
a few spicy details to make
the story better.

·264·

That your husband (or your kids) must never, ever invite people to stay for the weekend without getting clearance from you first.

·265·

What a fine idea it is, once you've started talking out a problem, to keep at it until it's settled.

•266•

The distress of being mistaken for your younger friend's mother.

•267•

Those hideous little pink lines that happen when lipstick bleeds.

·268·

Why you should think
twice before deciding to be
best friends with your daughter:
She's going to borrow (and ruin)
your favorite silk blouse, tell
you about her sex life, ask you
personal questions, and expect
you to hang out at the mall.

•269•

That ordering takeout for your
family's dinner may make you
feel guilty for forty-three seconds,
but you'll get over it.

•270•

There's no better, faster high
than a great haircut or blow-dry—
and nothing more depressing
than a bad one.

•271•

That using your period as
an excuse for work problems
(like lateness or uncompleted
projects) is a bad idea if you
want to get ahead.

•272•

How annoying it is when men bike, sprint, or climb to the top of the hill and then stand there waiting impatiently for you as if you're holding them back. Why did they invite you to come in the first place?

•273•

That skipping or missing a meal is not a federal disaster.

• 274 •

That you are very definitely your child's mother, but you are very definitely *not* your husband's mother.

• 275 •

That the busier you are, the more you can accomplish.

•276•

How to write a really good thank-you note or condolence note.

•277•

Why it's so hard to ask a man for a date. But only the first fifty times.

·278·

That behind your sunglasses
you're checking out

a) your reflection in the
store window

b) the buns of the cute guy
walking in front of you

c) the outfit on that woman
coming toward you

d) your reflection in the store
window—again

e) all of the above

• 279 •

Why women in certain
professions feel pressured
to have face-lifts.

That despite the fact that baby
boomer women are smart,
numerous, well-heeled,
and major consumers, advertisers
are not paying attention.

• 281 •

That the hour before everyone else gets up is the hour when you can get the most done.

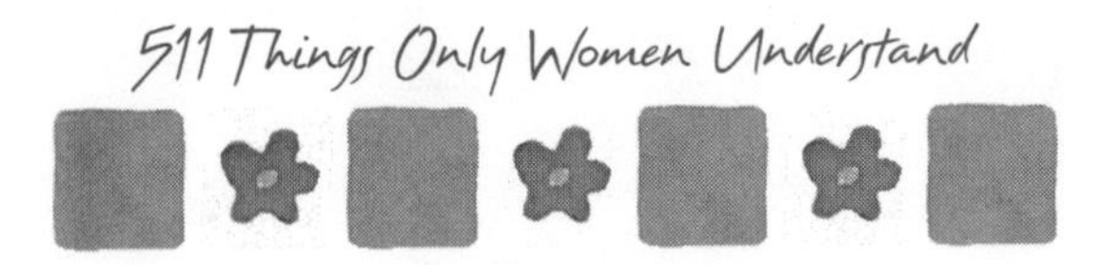

•282•

How to ask politely,
instead of giving orders.

How to wait patiently in a line.

•284•

How to be an Earth Mother.
Or not.

·285·

Hemlines.

·286·

That the boy who was too nice for his own good in high school is the man you want to reconnect with when you're thinking permanent.

• 287 •

The affront of the following
question, delivered by a maître d'
in a tone of scornful disbelief:
Table for one, madam?

Weird beauty products,
such as lip plumper, liquid powder
(an oxymoron), pore refiner, skin
refinisher, hair serum, eye primer.

· 289 ·

Getting completely dressed for a party, deciding that your outfit looks absolutely awful, taking it off, and starting from scratch.

· 290 ·

That if your mother, your best friend, *and* your pet hate the guy, he's not the one for you.

·291·

That it is a very serious offense to get in a ten-items-only express line with more than twelve items.

·292·

Why his collection of Hulk posters does not belong anywhere in your new house. Okay, maybe in the basement. Or in a dark closet with the door shut.

• 293 •

That friends are generous and invaluable sources of information about everything from soup stock to stock tips.

• 294 •

Why the tux he bought cheap in 1982 is unacceptable to wear to your niece's formal wedding next month at the Hotel Splendide.

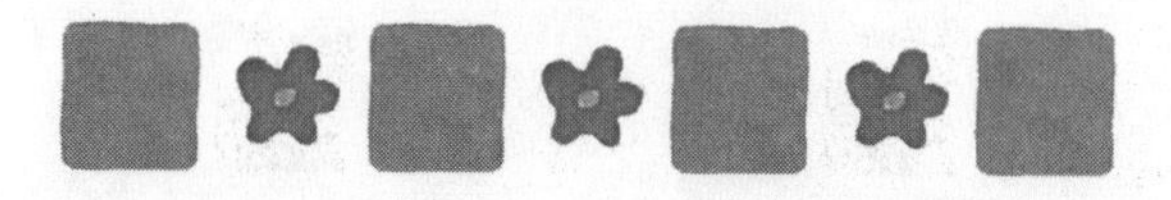

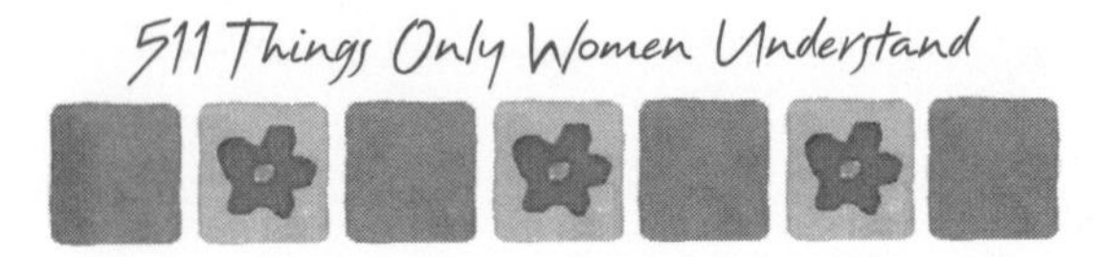

•295•

Feeling guilty for not doing enough and feeling guilty for doing too much.

Feeling guilty for feeling competitive and feeling guilty for wanting to get out of the race.

• 297 •

Having 237 cookbooks,
and not using any of them.

Exactly why it's heaven
to shop till you drop.

• 299 •

The fun, fun, fun of shaving
your legs and underarms,
and waxing your bikini line.

· 300 ·

That asking him to slow
down is not an all-out
attack on his driving ability.
You're just scared out of
your wits when the speedometer
hits ninety-five.

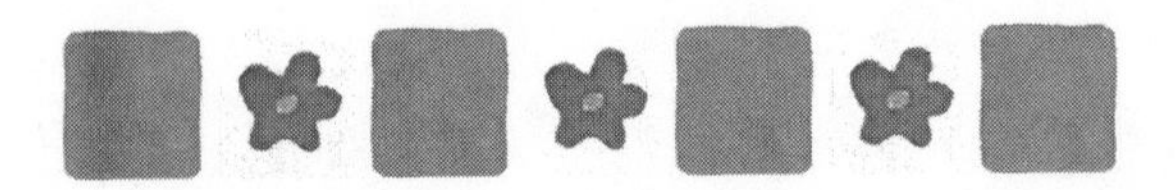

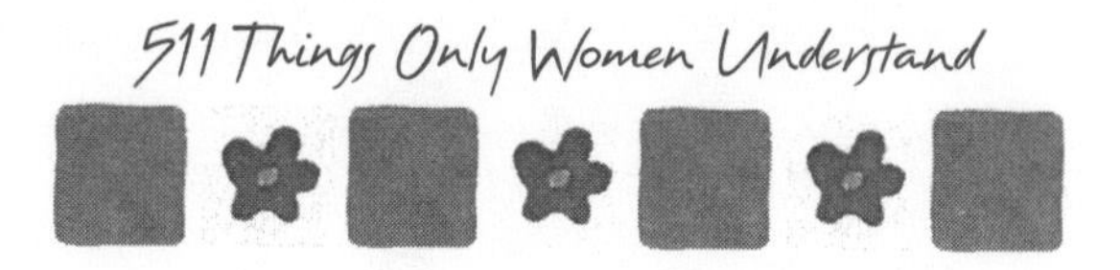

• 301 •

That women have been
mentoring each other for millennia,
without giving it the fancy name.
(Bulletin: Mentoring is now
standard operating procedure
in business.)

·302·

Why men get either wildly aggressive or totally passive in countries where they don't speak the language. Women, as you know, remain calm and reasonable.

·303·

That putting on a wedding ring does not automatically deactivate the flirting mechanism.

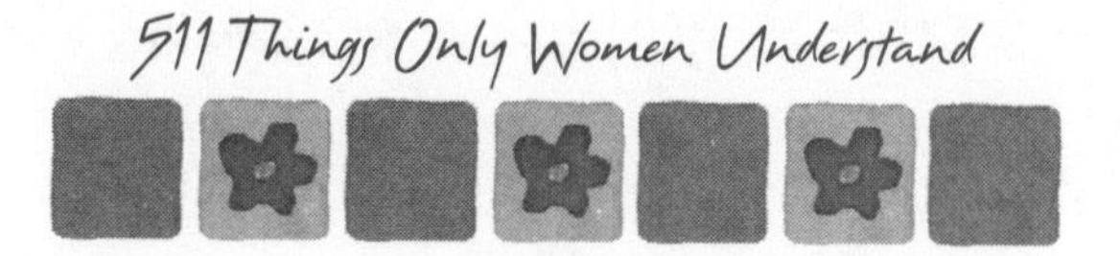

• 304 •

The cozy charm of afternoon tea served with little sandwiches and miniature pastries.

·305·

That on every dating
criteria list there are negotiables
(such as whether a person
favors stocks or bonds)
and nonnegotiables
(such as whether a person favors
chocolate or vanilla).

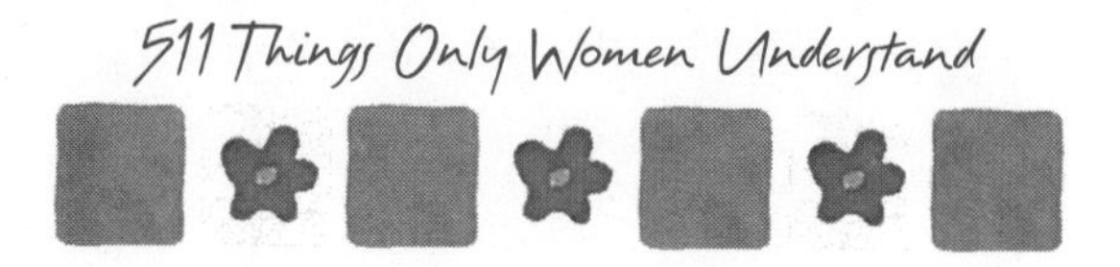

• 306 •

That not every item of clothing you buy is an item of clothing you're going to wear.

• 307 •

How boring it is for a non-mom
to listen to a mom chatter
endlessly about her baby and
everything related to it.

• 308 •

How infuriating it is for a mom
to listen to a non-mom dither
on about the boring details
of bad dates and job crises.

• 309 •

That performance anxiety (especially in bed) is not a males-only issue.

• 310 •

That sincerity trumps a smart-ass comeback every time.

•311•

The terms "good girl" and "bad girl" and why we resent them.

•312•

That if you shop for clothes when you're depressed, you'll be sorry.

· 313 ·

That men who like their
mothers and sisters probably
like women and are therefore
worth considering as
long-term propositions.

· 314 ·

The difference between
women's magazines
and real life.

•315•

Barbie.

•316•

Why you'd want to iron your hair.

•317•

That you can accomplish only a quarter of what you had planned to do on any single day.

• 318 •

Why you buy a cartload of new organizers—files, folders, boxes, shelves—when your life feels completely out of control.

• 319 •

That the longest lines at the supermarket are always on the day and at the time when you absolutely have to go there.

• 320 •

That a brand-new manicure in a bright new color can actually help chase the blues when therapy doesn't make a dent. Sometimes.

• 321 •

The heart-stopping moment when, after antiquing all day, you make the Big Find.

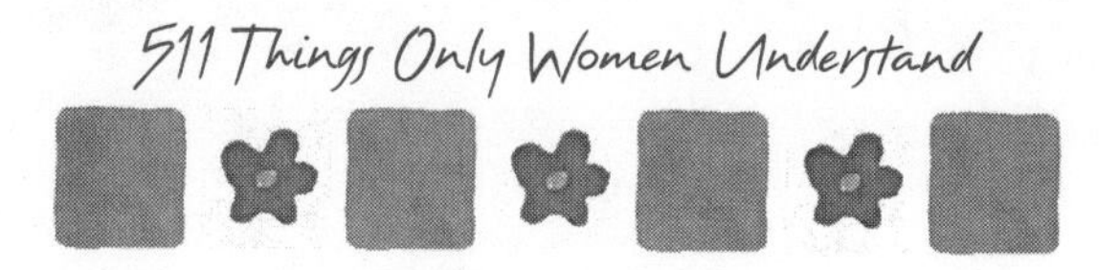

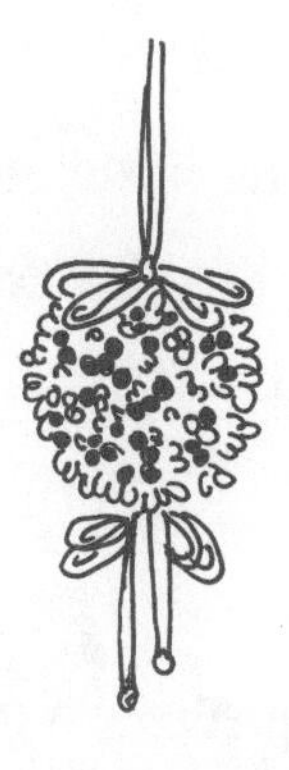

·322·

How romantic it is
to be kissed under
the mistletoe.

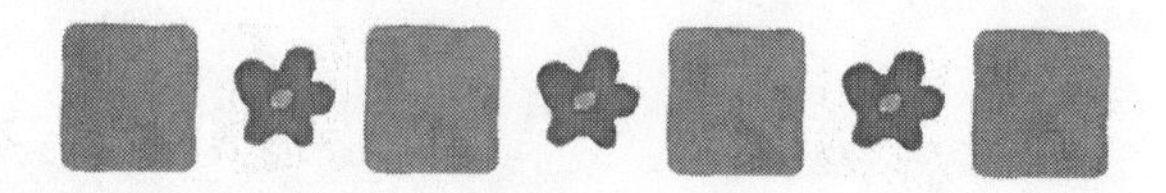

• 323 •

That the best time for
making love is *not* when

• you're totally exhausted from
being awake for thirty-six hours
straight with a sick baby

• you just saw a movie
starring Roberto Romance
and you're wishing you
were in Rome—alone

- you just got in on the red-eye and you haven't had a shower since yesterday morning
- you're involved, heart and soul, in a project that will make or break your career
- the movers are arriving in forty-five minutes

•324•

That surprise parties for women shouldn't be surprises. Who wants to throw open the rumpus room door and be caught in an old sweat suit and bunny slippers?

•325•

That life is a long-distance race, not a fifty-yard dash.

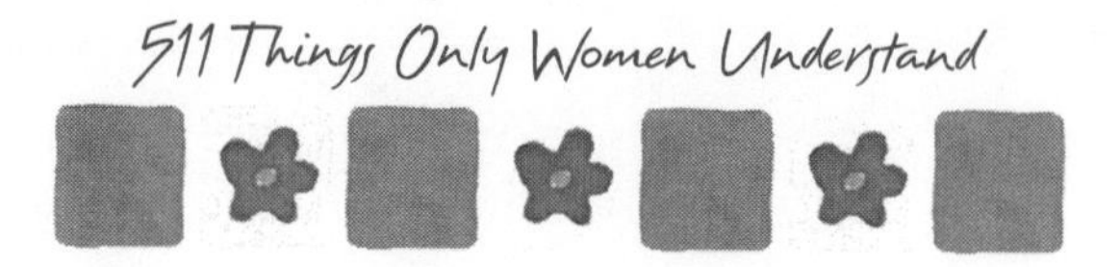

·326·

Needlepoint. Embroidery.
Crocheting. Knitting.

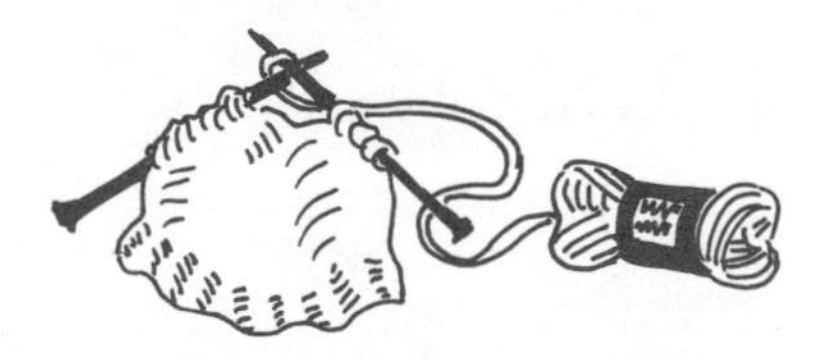

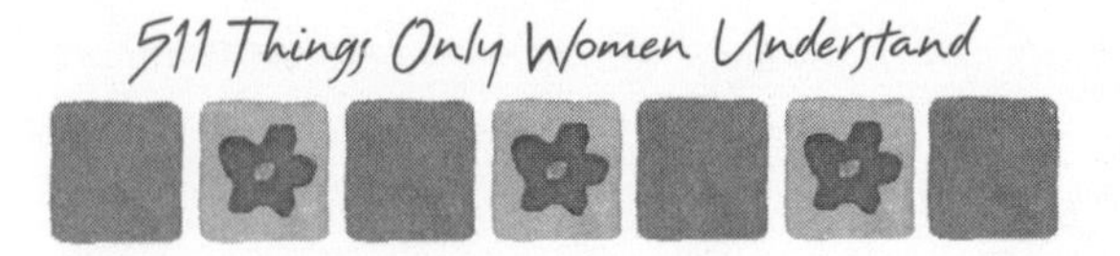

• 327 •

Crying at the movies.

• 328 •

Crying at weddings.

• 329 •

Crying in the shower.

• 330 •

Being incredibly organized
at work but totally disorganized
at home. Or vice versa.

• 331 •

That contrary to what the men's
magazines say, very few women are
actually turned on by supermuscled,
weight-lifter types. (Unless the
women are the supermuscled,
weight-lifter types, too.)

·332·

That contrary to popular mythology, the hours spent with your girlfriends are not unproductive or silly or fruitless or a waste of precious work time.

333

Why you're going to read
something you're not supposed
to read, like someone else's diary
or daybook: You might be in it.
(Okay, it's a disgraceful thing to do,
but why should that stop you?)

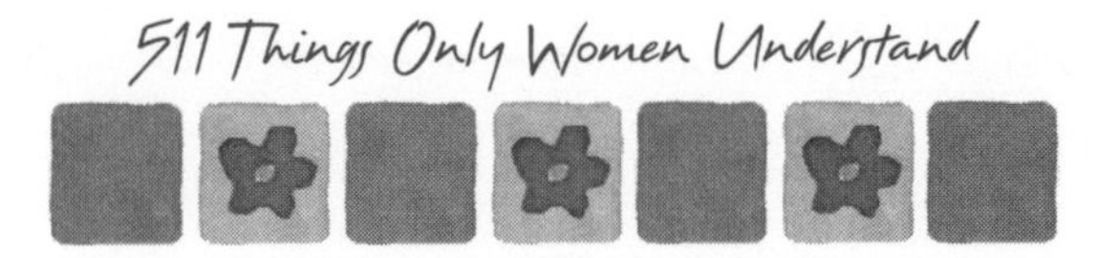

• 334 •

Spending $175 at the makeup counter, and never using any of the stuff you bought.

·335·

How to pick the *right* present.

·336·

That there's no point in saving that old purple-and-green shirtwaist dress, because when it finally comes back into style, it will look hideously dated instead of fashionably retro.

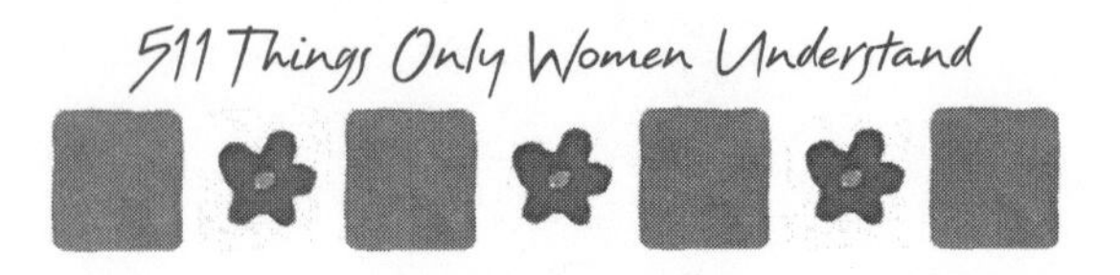

· 337 ·

That no matter what he says, condensed soup straight from the can, accompanied by a bag of chips and a beer, does not constitute a balanced meal.

· 338 ·

How to tell if he's been cheating.

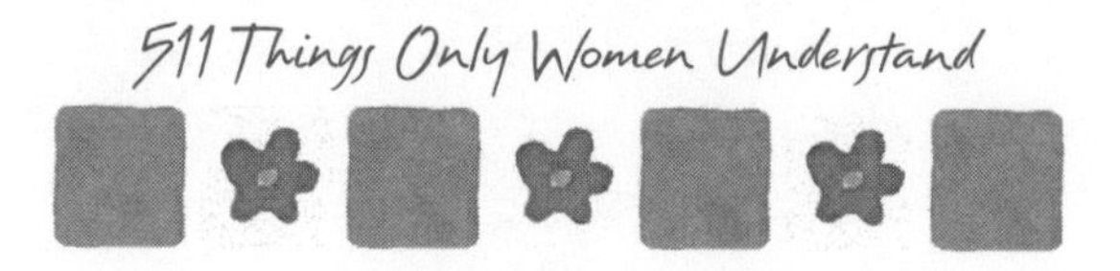

•339•

The excitement of polishing silver. When that tarnish disappears and the shine comes up . . . oh, mama.

•340•

The correct technique for giving advice. (Think Abby, Ann, and Heloise.)

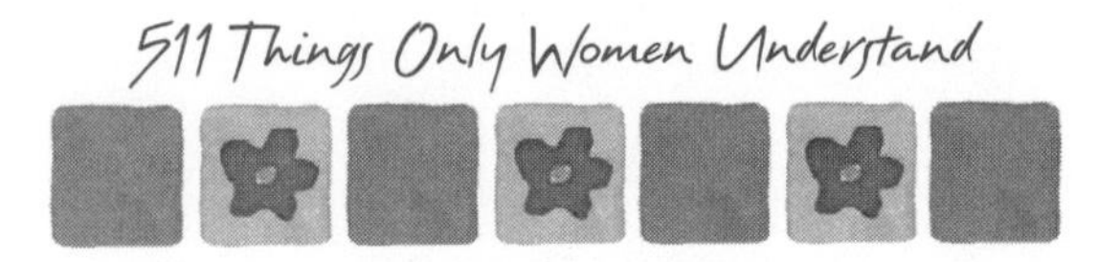

·341·

That the more you ask
a man to do something,
the less likely he is to do it.

That if it's something
he really doesn't want to do,
no amount of reminding him
will produce action.

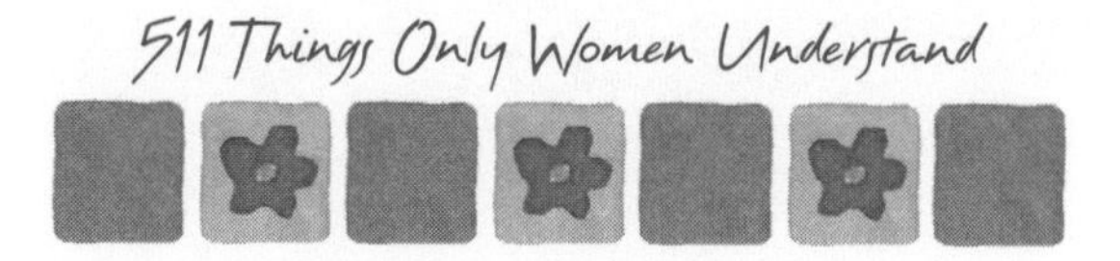

• 343 •

Why it's an ego saver to work out at home until you feel and look good enough to work out beside the buff ladies at the gym.

·344·

How to pass up the dessert cart in a restaurant: Make a dash for the ladies' room.

That when you reach a certain age, you're allowed to dress in weird outfits, wear fat running shoes, be a curmudgeon, and not give a damn.

• 346 •

The joy of being an aunt,
a grandmother, or a godmother.

Joni Mitchell. Carly Simon.
Carole King.

• 348 •

The freedom that comes
with menopause.

·349·

That even though you have never actually left on the oven, iron, coffeepot, or bathwater when leaving the house, the day you neglect to go back and check one last time will be the day you have indeed forgotten.

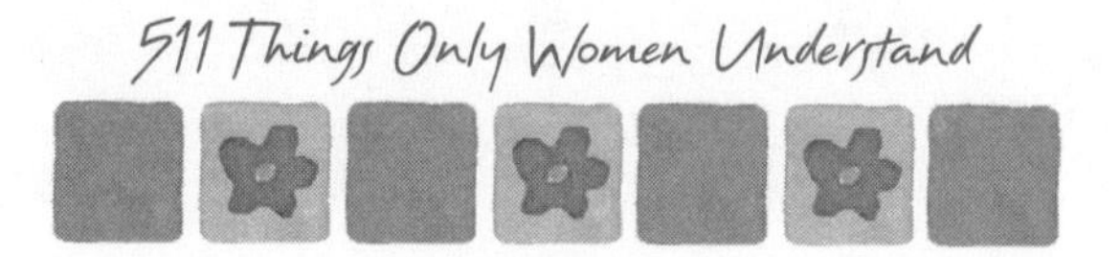

•350•

That empty-nest syndrome may be short-lived because your kids could be moving back home sooner than you think.

·351·

That you'd be eternally grateful if this year your husband would exchange his tight-and-tiny bikini bathing suit for a nice boxer style.

·352·

How to spend an entire day at home doing beauty things to your face and body and never get bored.

• 353 •

How to deal with the housekeeper.

• 354 •

That no matter what your husband or boyfriend thinks, your job is tougher than his.

• 355 •

The pleasure of poring through catalogs for hours at a time, even if you never order a thing.

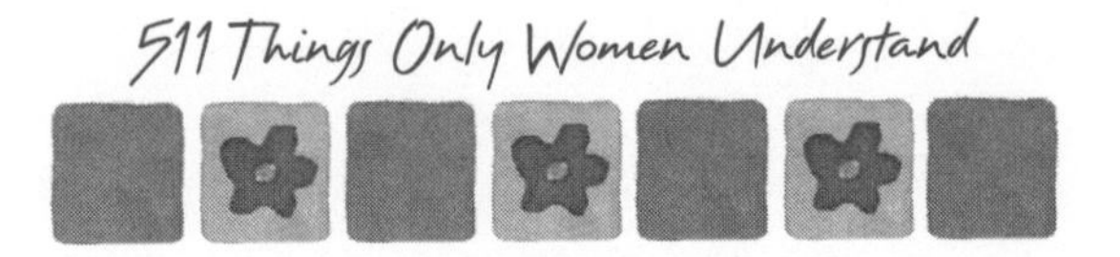

·356·

Why you want to sock him when he asks for your advice and doesn't take it.

How to tie a bow tie.

·358·

How to buy a sofa.

•359•

How to have a baby.

•360•

That making

a) matzo balls

b) spaghetti sauce

c) tuna casserole

d) fried chicken

e) all of the above

just like his mother's is not one of your lifetime goals.

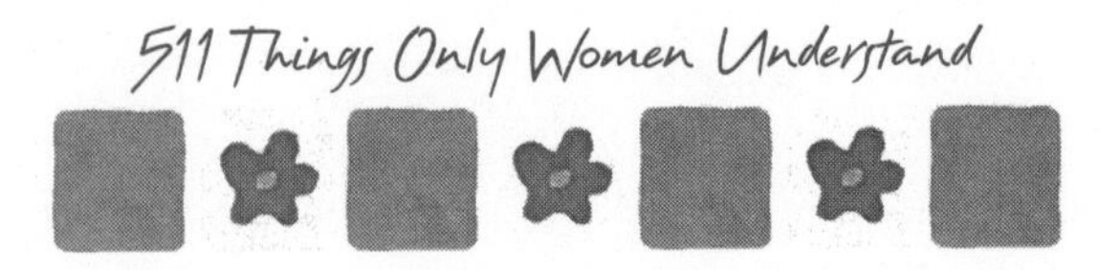

• 361 •

That it's okay to lie about
your weight and your age,
as long as you make the story
reasonably credible and
keep a straight face.

• 362 •

The fine art of
being a best friend.

·363·

That some major transgressions
can actually be atoned for—
with offerings of gold, silver,
platinum, or precious stones.

•364•

Housewarming gifts.

•365•

Why it takes a minimum
of five products to
make up your face.

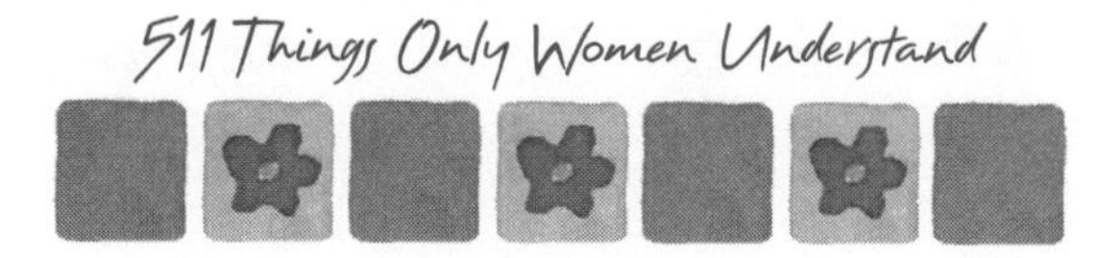

• 366 •

The terror of a nearly empty parking lot at night, when your car is right next to a van with blacked-out windows. (And you'd *never* go to your car without a security guard, right?)

• 367 •

That it's not fun to talk to an open newspaper across the table at breakfast.

•368•

That when you get sullen and silent, you want him to ask you what's wrong.

And when he asks you what's wrong, you don't expect him to fix it. You just want to be held and told that everything's going to be okay.

·370·

Why it's nice to dance with a partner: It's relaxing to let someone else lead for a change.

• 371 •

That you *should* be able to wear anything you want at your job and still be taken seriously, but we're not there yet.

·372·

That a lot of men are convinced that women are bad at math and science, silly about money, too emotional, scaredy-cats, and not tough enough. This from folks who can't figure out how the copier works, don't know how to comparison-shop, get hysterical over the Cubs, are terrified by the IRS, and cave in to whatever their mothers want. Nice try, guys.

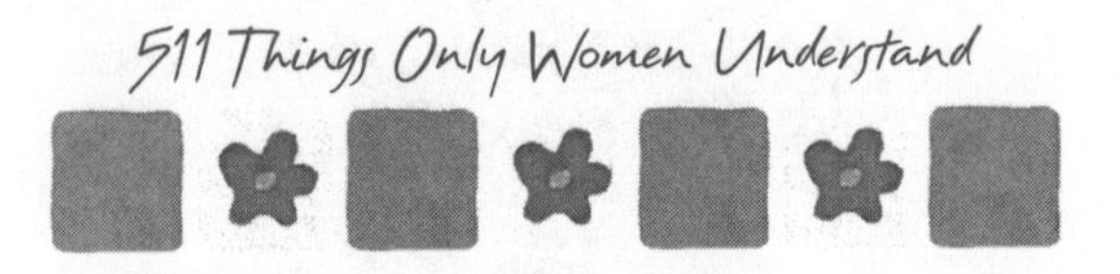

•373•

Why the question
What's for dinner, Mom?
will be the last question you'll
answer before packing your
bags and absconding to Tahiti.

• 374 •

Talisman clothes: the dress that always brings luck at job interviews, the sweater that always gets the guy, the necklace that always gives you power.

• 375 •

Listening to all the mundane details of your best girlfriend's life, and telling her all the mundane details of yours.

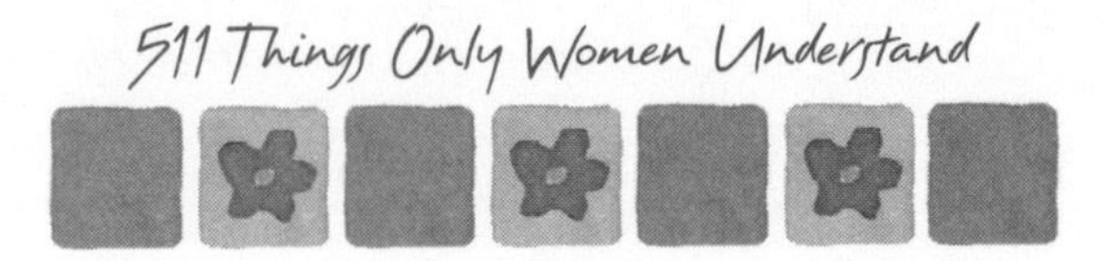

• 376 •

Bubble baths.

• 377 •

That the most important sex organ is the brain.

• 378 •

Why snoring is grounds for divorce.

•379•

That spending a Sunday cooking and freezing meals for the coming week is a waste of a perfectly good Sunday. (Just roast a pair of chickens on Monday and forget about it.)

•380•

What your friend really means when she says, Oh, please don't bother

a) helping with the dishes

b) bringing dessert

c) having her slipcover dry-cleaned after you've spilled red wine all over it

d) visiting her in the hospital

e) telephoning to find out how she's doing after her significant other has walked out

·381·

How to get out of any date
you regret having accepted:
Plead a bad case of cramps.

That *gossip* is just
another word for being
interested in people.

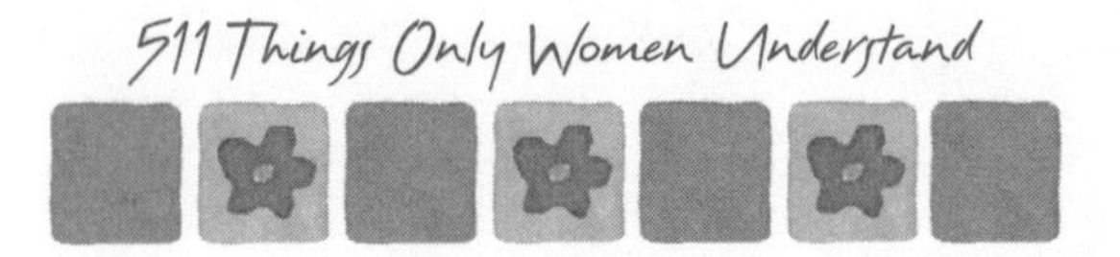

•383•

That no matter how much progress women have made, TV anchorwomen still have to be pretty and TV anchormen don't.

•384•

The difference between *discomfort* and *pain,* especially as it pertains to childbirth.

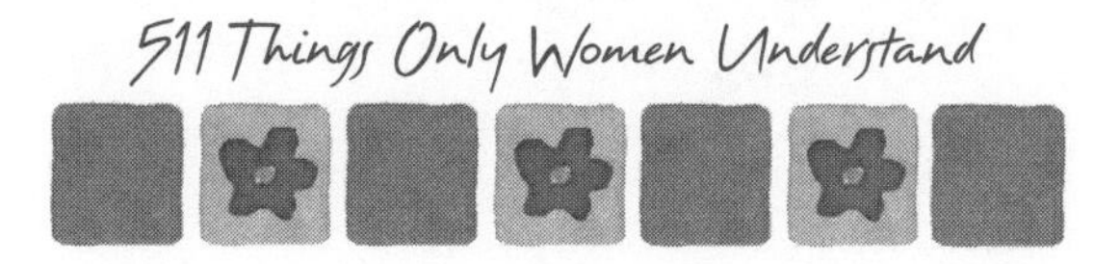

•385•

Certain women:

Eleanor Roosevelt

Gloria Steinem

Whoopi Goldberg

Vanna White

Janet Reno

Martha Stewart

Barbara Walters

Tina Turner

Lily Tomlin

·386·

The smartest time-saver of all: When you need a new vacuum cleaner, alarm system, computer, massage therapist, or anything else, don't bother doing research. Just ask the savvy woman who's recently acquired one.

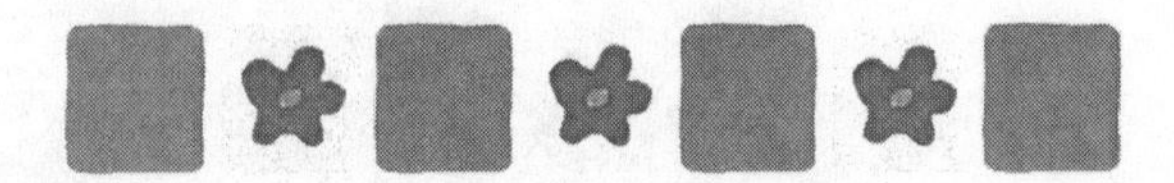

• 387 •

The concept of matching china, matching flatware, matching glasses.

• 388 •

Eating disorders: Whether you have one or not, you can feel for those who do.

·389·

Vulnerability:
Guess what, guys—
it won't kill you.

Cuddling: It's not a dirty word.

·391·

That there's no such thing as an efficient recipe-saving system. No matter how many clever little folders and cute little boxes you buy, the recipes you clip from the Wednesday paper will still end up tucked into a cookbook, never to be found again.

·392·

Chin burn. Ouch.

·393·

That ten minutes after an argument is not a good time for sex. Except sometimes.

That when your teenager first gets her license, she'll be happy to do all the errands that require driving. Seize the moment.

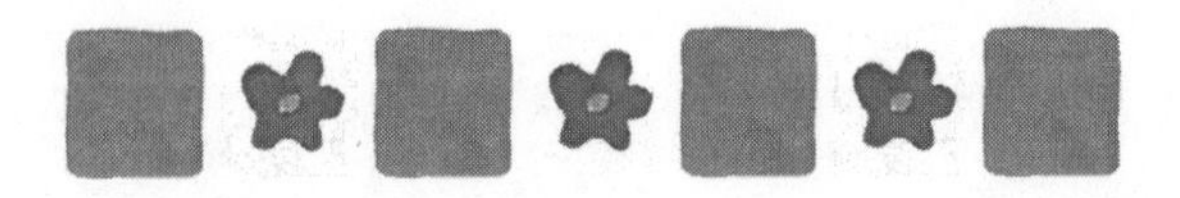

•395•

The difference between good eye contact between a man and a woman . . . and leering.

•396•

How to be a good listener.

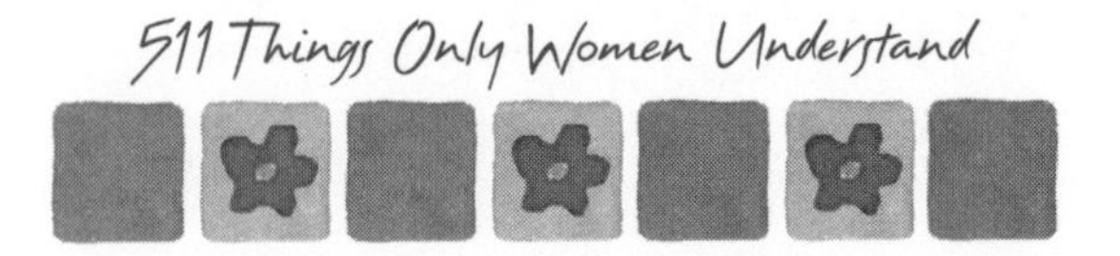

·397·

How to bake chocolate chip cookies. And nothing else.

·398·

Never to give your mother a key to your apartment.

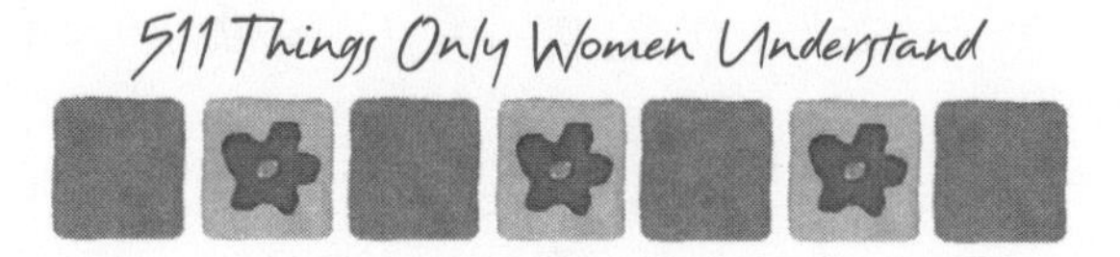

• 399 •

Romance novels.
Romance book clubs.
Romance cable channels.

• 400 •

That it's wrong to snoop
through your lover's stuff.
Which doesn't mean you're
not going to do it.

• 401 •

The jargon of underpants: thong, string thong, full seat coverage, bikini, hipster, full briefs, boy briefs.

• 402 •

That it is not amusing when your college-age kids leave their laundry for you to do.

• 403 •

That it is not amusing when your high-school-age kids leave their dishes for you to wash.

• 404 •

That it is not amusing when your elementary-school-age kids leave their toys lying around for you to pick up.

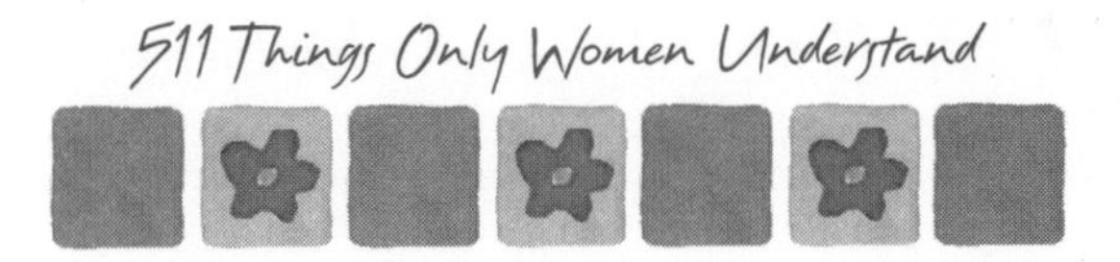

·405·

The correct responses to your most important questions:

You: How do you like my haircut?
Him: It's great.

You: Don't you just adore my mother?
Him: She's terrific.

You: Does this make me look fat?
Him: You look perfect.

You: Do you love me?
Him: Eternally.

• 406 •

How much fun it is to discuss Great Meals You Have Eaten while you're eating a great meal.

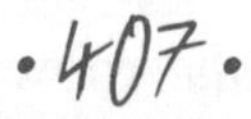

The difference between a teddy, a camisole, a bustier, and a body stocking.

·408·

How infuriating it is when your single friend gives your husband a disapproving glare if he doesn't offer to help with the dishes. How does *she* know what your arrangement is? For all she knows he's been up all night with the baby.

·409·

How infuriating it is when your husband teases your single friend about her track record with relationships. How does *he* know what's really going on in her life?

·410·

The correct techniques for organizing a closet, shelf, drawer, file cabinet, or Rolodex.

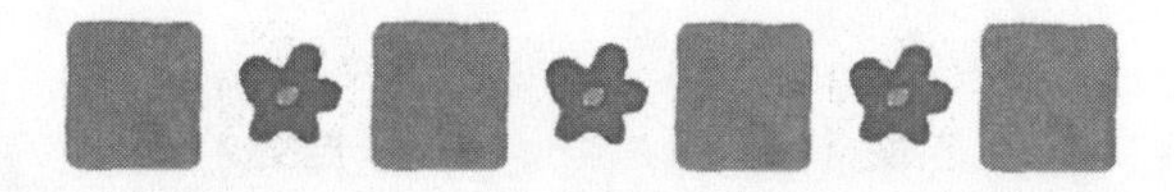

• 411 •

That we actually use only 5 percent of the cooking equipment in our kitchen cabinets. The other 95 percent is there to aid and abet the fantasy that someday when we have time we'll make ravioli, bake popovers, and decorate cakes.

That the real reasons for buying the newspaper are the horoscope, the business section, and the obituaries.

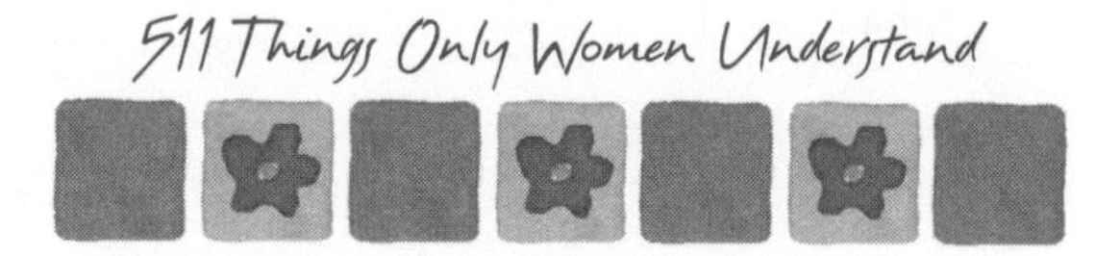

• 413 •

That washing the lettuce is the world's most boring chore.

• 414 •

That when you pull back from a relationship, he suddenly gets more interested. Go figure.

• 415 •

The blessing of children: They can be used as excuses to get you out of almost anything you don't want to do.

· 416 ·

What can go (safely) in the dryer.

· 417 ·

Why an occasional compliment about your brains would be appreciated, interspersed with all those remarks about your body.

·418·

How many lovers are
too many lovers.

·419·

That buying something new
can boost your spirits almost as
much as winning the lottery.

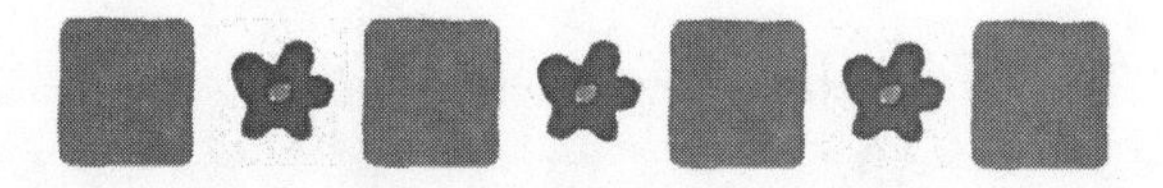

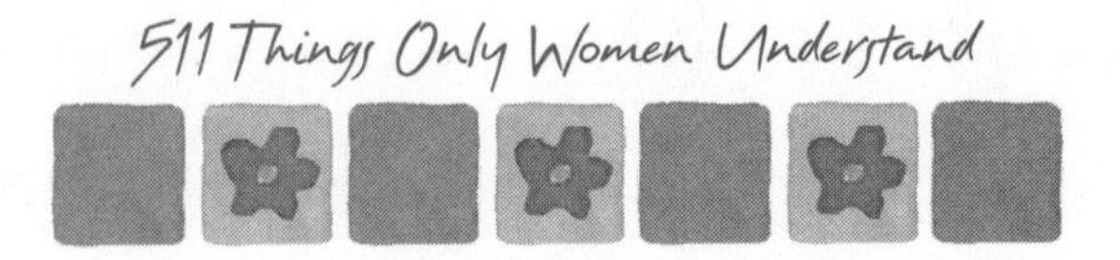

• 420 •

When to throw out that

• old head of lettuce

• pair of sneakers so worn that the soles are perfectly smooth

• stack of two-year-old newspapers

• string of love beads

• yucky, shredded sponge

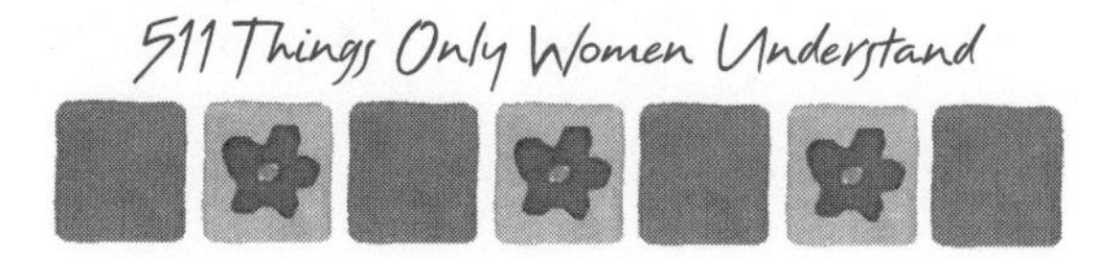

• 421 •

How disappointing it is that he doesn't remember every earth-shaking moment of your romance as well as you do.

• 422 •

That weighing yourself three times a day certainly does *not* mean you're obsessed with your weight.

• 423 •

That you must never cry
(in public) at work.

How to be a good patient.

·425·

That the best day-to-day time-saver is to cut your hair short (so it takes no time to fix) or let it grow long (so you can let it hang loose, shove it on top of your head, or stick it in a ponytail). It's the in-between lengths that gobble up the hours.

• 426 •

How offensive it is to be called a wallflower, a spinster, or an old maid—these labels disparage a woman specifically because she doesn't have a man.

• 427 •

How offensive it is to women when a man is called a weak sister, an old woman, or a sissy—these labels disparage a man by comparing him unfavorably to a woman.

•428•

The thrill of taking your daughter to work with you.

•429•

Passing a handful of toilet paper under the partition to your girlfriend in the next-door stall.

•430•

Wrapping your coat tightly over your entire head so you can't see or hear anything until the scary part of the movie is over.

•431•

Fitting room etiquette. (Don't ask, don't tell.)

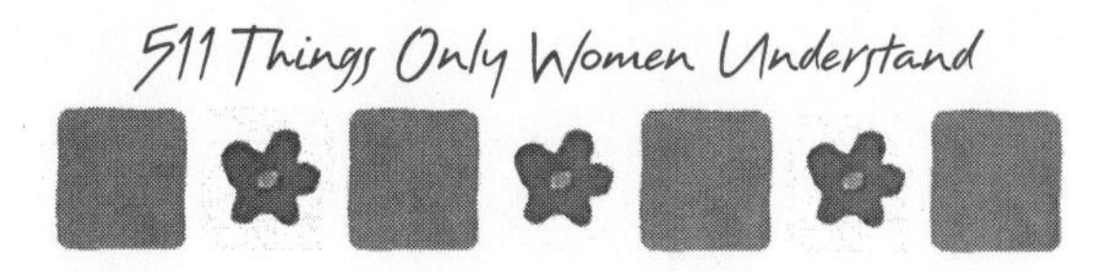

• 432 •

Stuffed animals.

• 433 •

That cheating is cheating, whether it's a one-hour lunch date or the whole enchilada.

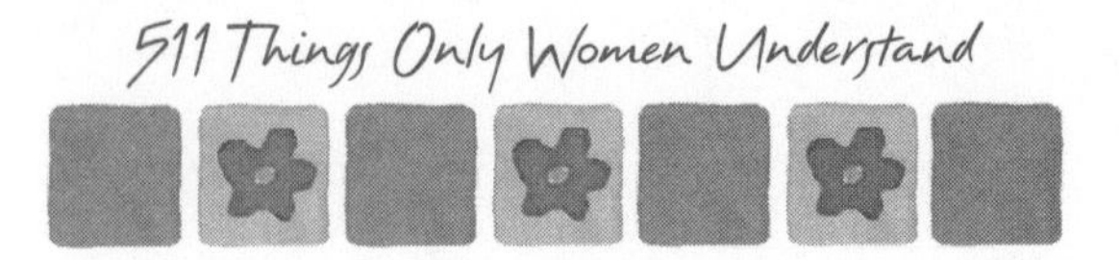

•434•

That there is very little charm in finding a pile of damp towels on the bathroom floor after your significant other has finished his beauty routine.

•435•

Why certain remarks that men are allowed to make to each other (such as "One more piece of pizza and you'll turn into a blimp") must never be said to a woman.

•436•

That red is a neutral color.

·437·

That wearing his cologne is almost as good as having him near you when you have to be apart for a day, a week, a month.

·438·

The arguments for and against tummy tucks and liposuction.

• 439 •

That when you want to know what's really going on in any given social situation, don't bother asking a man.

• 440 •

That there's no acceptable excuse for failing to RSVP.

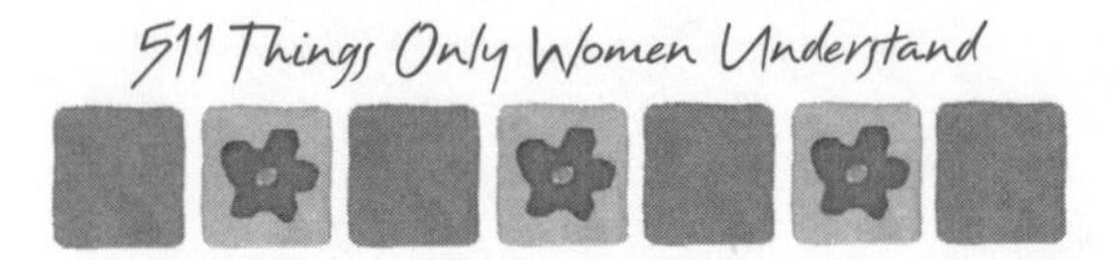

·441·

That the snacks you pluck from the shelves and munch while doing the grocery shopping don't count when you're adding up the calories. Neither do the cookie crumbs in the bottom of the box.

• 442 •

The value of speaking in complete sentences instead of grunts and monosyllables.

• 443 •

That you must keep a stash of at least a hundred bucks hidden (not too hidden) at home for emergencies. Someday you'll be glad you did.

·444·

Why it's often hard
to be confrontational
in a bad situation.

·445·

Superniceness.

·446·

That insecurity is the
opposite side of arrogance.

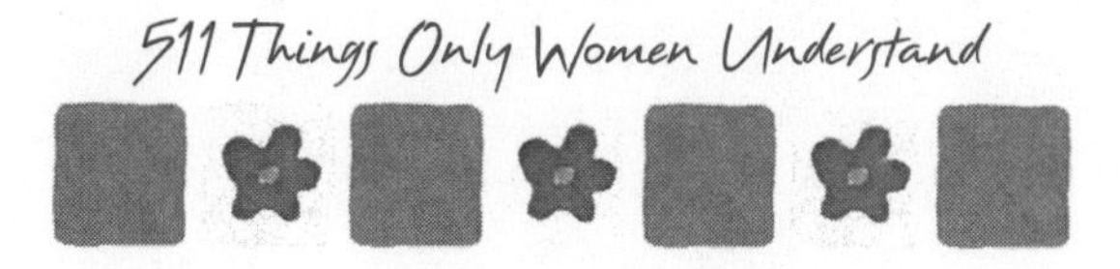

• 447 •

Certain drinks:

kir royale
cosmopolitan
Bellini
whiskey sour
pink Russian
champagne cocktail

• 448 •

That even though the organizing fanatics would like you to believe you'll save time by doing one of your morning chores (such as making the school lunches) the night before, you won't actually save a minute: It takes the same amount of time to do it at night, and it just makes you even more exhausted.

• 449 •

That deodorant is
as essential as air.

• 450 •

When he should stop trying to plug
the leak, rewire the walls, repair
the roof, fix the boiler, or
replace the tiles—and call
a professional, for
heaven's sake.

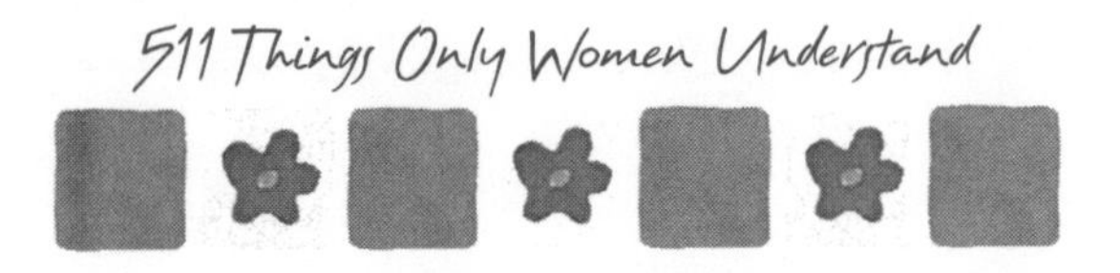

• 451 •

How we've been brainwashed
to repeat the mantra
If only I were thinner . . .

• 452 •

That even if he hates
holding hands and kissing
in public, he'll have to learn
to live with them.

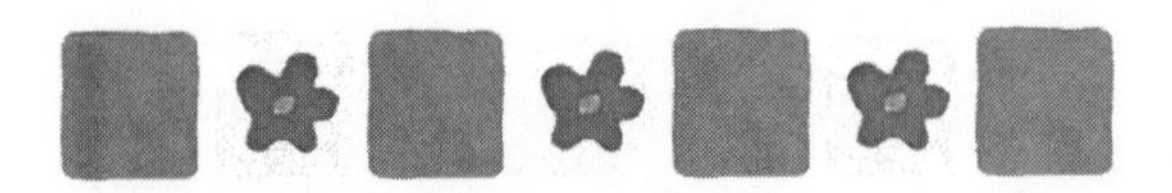

• 453 •

How lucky we are that we don't have to wear suits and ties to the office day after day after day after day.

• 454 •

How unnerving it is to have your body parts scrutinized while you're attempting to engage in a friendly flirtation.

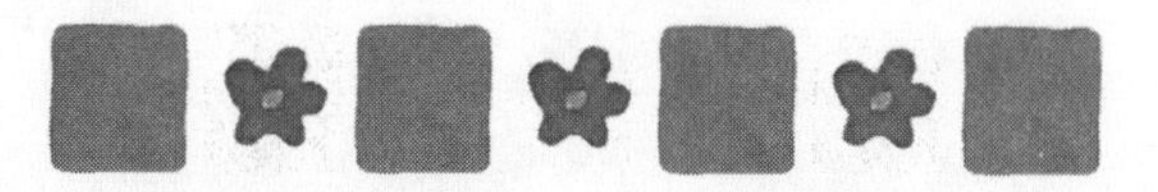

·455·

That you're allowed to skip the boring parts of a book. And read the last page first.

·456·

That if your girlfriend's husband makes a pass at you in the back hallway during a party, you mustn't tell her. He'll deny it, and she'll be furious—at you.

• 457 •

How dispiriting it is to spend five hours preparing a meal that will be gobbled up in thirty minutes.

That when you meet a new person, it's generally considered good manners to smile and be friendly instead of scowling, shifting from foot to foot, and looking for the nearest exit door.

• 459 •

Housecleaning Rule No. 1:
Start in a different room each time.
That way at least the first room gets
a thorough cleaning before you
poop out on the second room.
Better yet, hire a housekeeper.

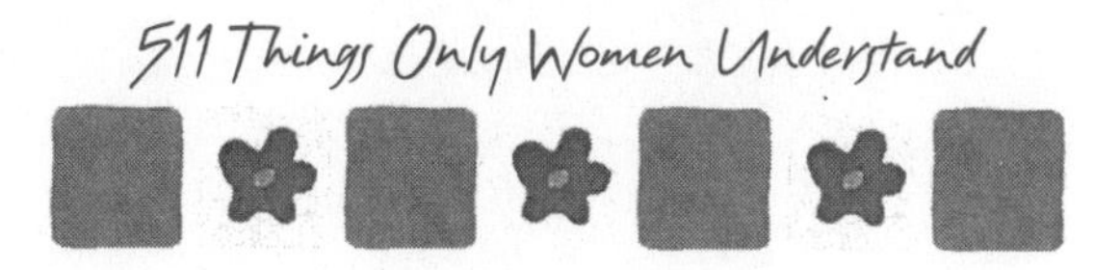

• 460 •

That too much aftershave is worse than none at all.

• 461 •

The pleasure of sharing clothes with your sister or girlfriend.

• 462 •

Photo albums.

463

The postrelationship cycle of disbelief, rage, revenge, relapse, and recovery.

That we're rarely paid what we're worth. There probably isn't enough money in the Department of the Treasury to cover that tab.

•465•

There's no such thing as
too many compliments.

•466•

When you're out with friends,
there's only one way to avoid
eating something that's not on your
current diet: Tell the gang you have
a food allergy so bad that if you
even touch the cream sauce,
you'll swell up like an air mattress.

• 467 •

Why it is an immutable law
of nature that when you look
absolutely awful you will run into

a) your worst female enemy

b) your mother-in-law

c) the guy who stood
you up in 1998

d) the guy you've been
flirting with at work

e) all of the above

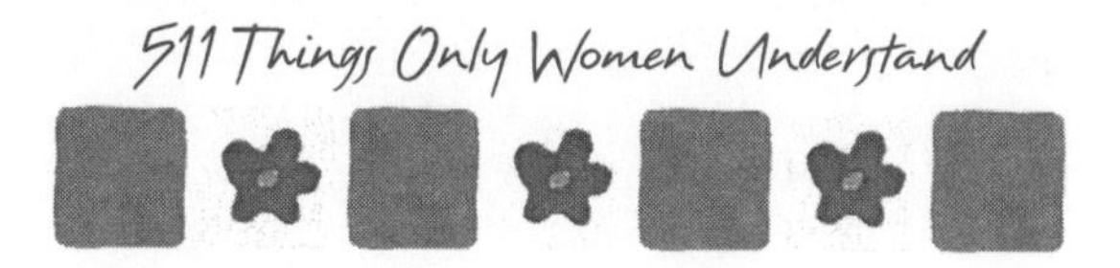

·468·

Not to interrupt another person when he or she is speaking. (Ever notice who does most of the interrupting in any given conversation?)

·469·

How to use the person-to-person skills you learned on the playground—in the boardroom.

•470•

That what men say is more important than how they look.

How easy it is to be sucked into believing whatever your mother or sister thinks about you—good or bad.

•472•

That there's no excuse, none whatsoever, for the verbal or physical abuse of women by men.

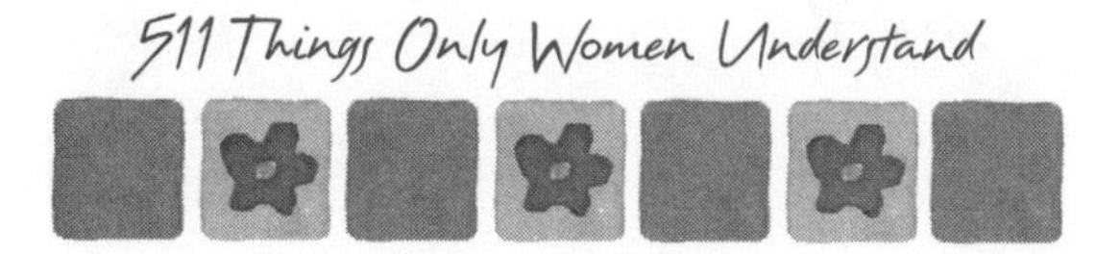

•473•

That there's no excuse, none whatsoever, for deadbeat dads.

How demoralizing it is to realize you are but one in the flock of style sheep.

•475•

How to ask for directions.

• 476 •

How to nurture friendships.

• 477 •

That marrying you does
not automatically excuse
a man from courting you.

• 478 •

How to eliminate all fat from the diet.

• 479 •

Glamour.

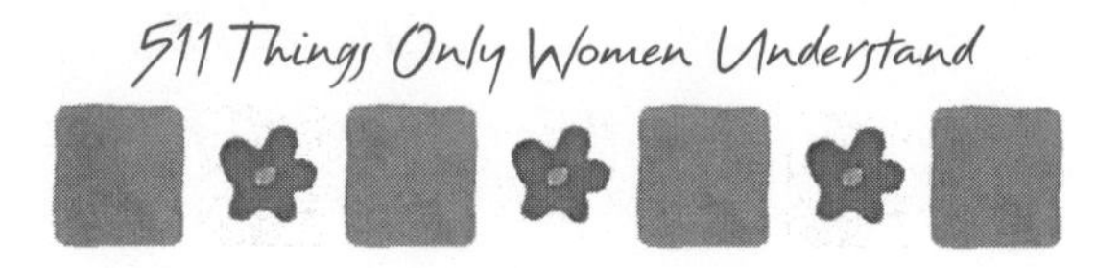

• 480 •

How much time and effort
it actually takes to

- sort the laundry
- do the food shopping
- keep track of the family social calendar
- balance the checkbook
- weed the garden
- paint the kitchen

·481·

The right moment to be girlish. It's not at the sales meeting.

That crow's feet and gray hair are attractive in men, and signs of aging in women.

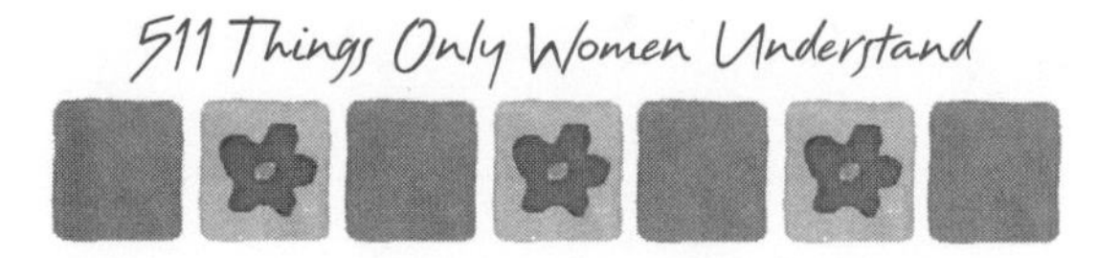

•483•

That your handbag is your portable intensive-care unit.

•484•

Why you want to breast-feed. Or why you don't.

·485·

That he must go with you to buy furniture because if he doesn't, three months later he'll tell you he hates the dining room table—and it will be *all your fault.*

·486·

That it's better to be happy than right. Or is it the other way around?

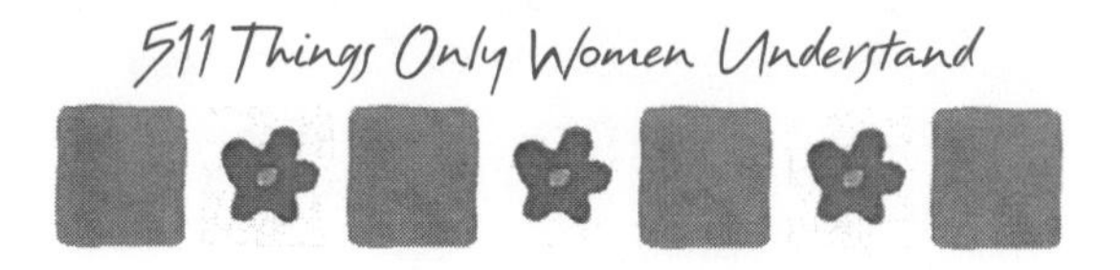

· 487 ·

When to confess and when to keep mum. Confession is good for the soul, but it may not be the best thing for the relationship. At least, not today.

· 488 ·

How uncomfortable it can be to sit alone at a bar.

• 489 •

That men invariably make instructions and information more complicated than they need to be. Moral: If you need instructions or information, ask a woman.

• 490 •

The itsy-bitsy quarter inch of extra flesh that turns a snug pair of pants into a too-tight pair of pants.

• 491 •

Pressure cookers.

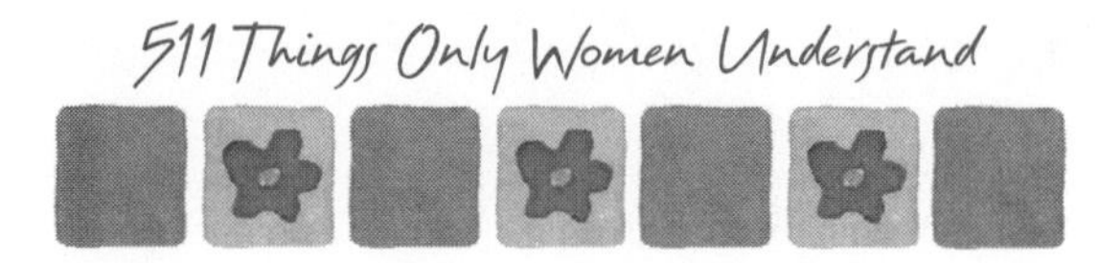

• 492 •

The correct home remedies for

- cramps (a pussycat on your stomach)
- headache (a neck-and-scalp rub)
- backache (a full body massage)
- stomachache (never eating again in your life)
- muscle ache (more of whatever gave you the ache in the first place, except housework)

·493·

The difference between sexy and trashy.

That your particular skills at communication, teamwork, and empathy can make you a far better manager than a man, when you get (or take) the chance.

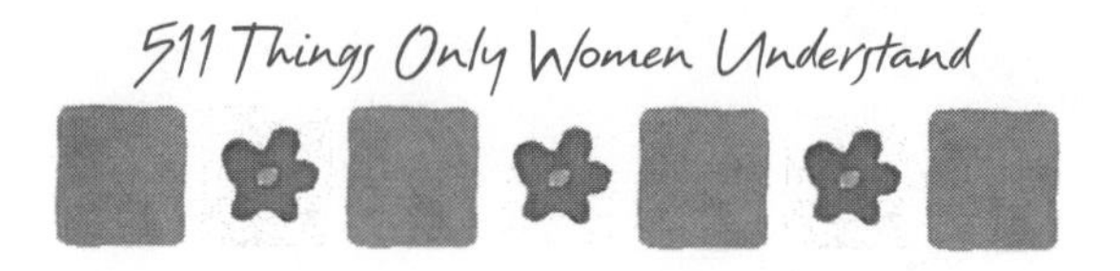

·495·

That—hello!—there's more than one person in every relationship.

The two most important reasons for having a little packet of tissues at all times: bursting into tears and public bathrooms with no toilet paper.

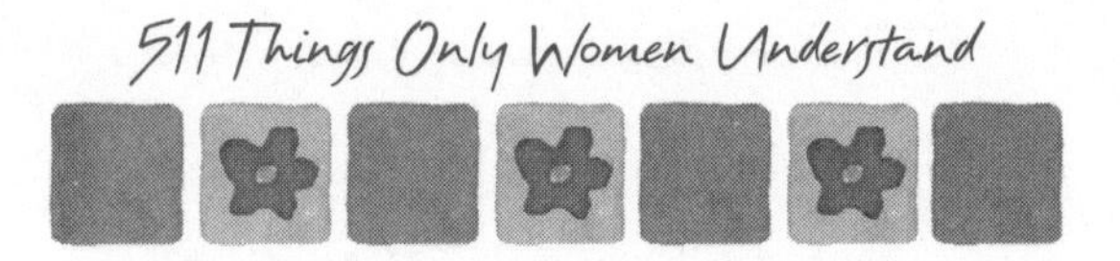

• 497 •

That we struggled through the women's movement so our daughters, granddaughters, and nieces could live in a world in which they'd wonder why we ever had to have a women's movement.

•498•

That it's impossible to own
too much good jewelry.
Or even too much bad jewelry.

•499•

The appeal of a man
who isn't afraid to cry.

• 500 •

That you could probably get along without him if you had to, but he couldn't conceivably get along without you.

• 501 •

How to arrive at a sensible solution to any problem: by discussing every possible option, and if that fails, by sulking until you get your way.

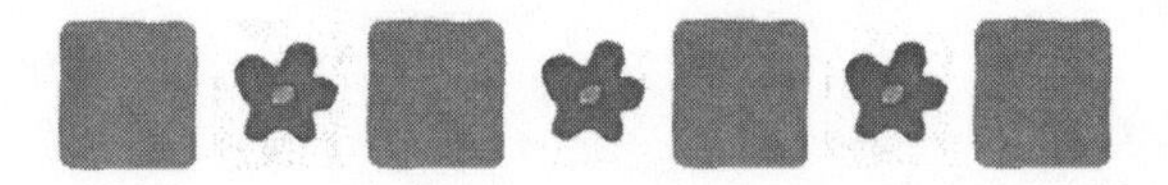

• 502 •

How hard it can be to choose
between staying at home with the
baby and going back to work.

That if you cozy up to him,
stroke his cheek, nibble his ear,
and unknot his tie,
you mean business.

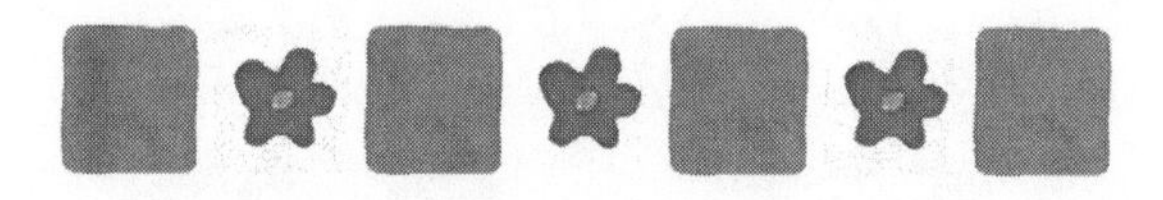

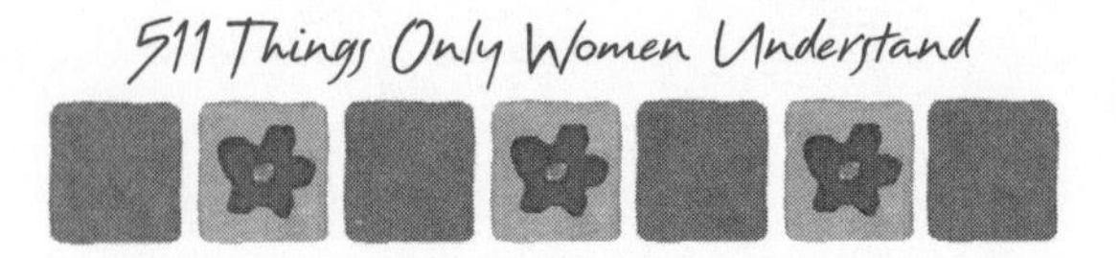

• 504 •

Birthdays. Anniversaries.
Valentine's Day.

Very small dogs.

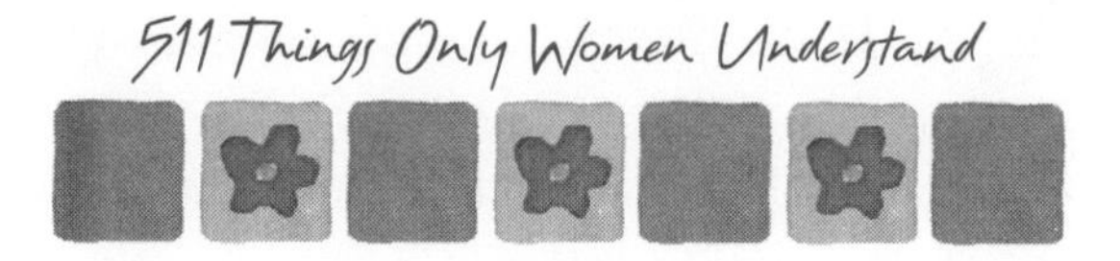

·506·

Nancy Drew.

·507·

Pajama parties.

·508·

The many meanings
of the double standard.

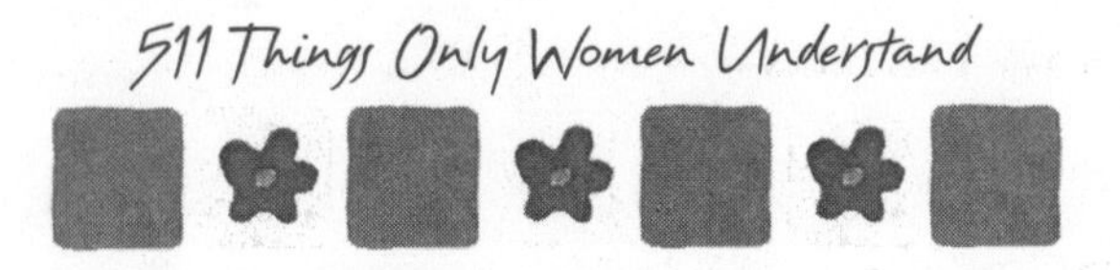

• 509 •

How to share a secret.
And how to keep one.

How to listen for the story
behind the story.

• 511 •

How to be perfect.